HIP**HOUSEPLANTS**

HIP**HOUSEPLANTS**

ORLANDO HAMILTON
PHOTOGRAPHY BY JEREMY HOPLEY

DK

LONDON, NEW YORK, SYDNEY, DELHI,
PARIS, MUNICH and JOHANNESBURG

Project Editor **Neil Lockley**
Senior Art Editor **Wendy Bartlet**
Category Publisher **Judith More**
Art Director **Janis Utton**
US Editors **Jane Perlmutter, Ray Rogers**
Horticultural Consultant **Andrew Mikolajski**
Contributor **Lynn Bryan**
Stylist **Wei Tang**
Production Controller **Louise Pope**
DTP Designer **Sonia Charbonnier**

Published in the United States by
DK Publishing, Inc., 95 Madison Avenue
New York, NY 10016

First American Edition, 2001
2 4 6 8 10 9 7 5 3 1

Copyright © 2001 Dorling Kindersley Limited

DK books are available at special discounts for bulk
purchases for sales promotions or premiums. Special
editions, including personalized covers and corporate
imprints, can be created in large quantities for specific
needs. For more information, contact Special Markets
Department, DK Publishing, Inc., 95 Madison Avenue,
New York, NY 10016 Fax: 800-600-9098.

Library of Congress Cataloging-in-Publication Data

Hamilton, Orlando.
  Hip houseplants/Orlando Hamilton;photography by
Jeremy Hopley.
    p. cm.
  ISBN 0-7894-8030-1 (alk. paper)
  1. Houseplants. 1. Title.

  SB419 H274 2001
  635965-dc21
                                2001028348

Reproduced by Colourscan Overseas Co. Pte. Ltd.,
Singapore
Printed and bound by LEGO, Italy

see our complete catalog at
www.dk.com

CONTENTS

FOREWORD

It may seem odd that I use the word "Hip" in conjunction with "houseplants," because to some readers they appear to be incompatible. However, I believe that houseplants are ready for a deserved comeback and when chosen carefully can play a pivotal role in modern interior decorating. This book aims to show how the right choice of plant and container will make an invaluable contribution to enhancing and defining your living space.

For me, the adventure with plants and flowers started at boarding school, where I had my own garden and grew my own fruit and vegetables. Several years later, while working in London, I was invited by a lady called Jennifer d'Abo to join her very prestigious flowershop. After leaving school, my initial interest in growing plants had waned, and I was probably as likely as the next person to buy my flowers at the supermarket. Although it seemed like a complete volte-face, I accepted the offer, and there started my new love affair with the horticultural world.

I am aware that the idea of cultivating plants indoors can be a daunting one, and I occasionally encounter people who regard themselves as serial houseplant killers. For them I have included plants that are low-maintenance and fall into what I call the "Terminator" category – difficult to kill. But there are also plants for the more adventurous that require love and attention.

Plants indoors are good for the soul (whether by their color or scent). Plants can be soothing or they can lift the spirits, but their most valuable benefit is that they can deliver style. I hope that *Hip Houseplants* will show you why they are always worthy of their inclusion in our homes.

Orlando Hamilton.

STYLES

LUXURIOUS MINIMALISM

Simplicity is the main aspect of this Zenlike approach to interior design. Its influence on the Western approach to creating a home is far-reaching.

The minimalist message is: keep only what is essential and elegant; clear out the clutter. The result will be a calm, harmonious living space.

This ideal would seem to rule out using plants for decoration, yet this is exactly the environment where a stunning plant like the moth orchid (*Phalaenopsis*) can make a luxurious contribution to a room. Its narrow stems allow light to filter through and its style is no-frills elegance. The winglike shape of its beautiful blooms is responsible for its name, and also its visual appeal, since its sprays arch enticingly for most of the year. It likes the sun, but not too bright; and dislikes a draft. Ideal for a centraly heated environment, the moth orchid will flower as long as it is watered every two weeks. Too much water upsets it, so do not saturate its epiphytic orchid soil mix.

Choose a container that will echo the slender lines of this plant. A smooth, satinlike surface would reflect the soft texture of its blooms; a tall container is best for a full-grown specimen. Oriental-style pots — either in highly lacquered or mat ceramic finishes — are an excellent choice, since they reflect the minimalist mood. Arrange the containers in a group to make a theatrical statement: a confident line of identical orchids or stiff-leaved plants — aloes or sansevierias, perhaps — parading along a windowsill or tabletop will strike the right note for disciplined minimalism.

Add a second indulgent note with interesting foliage. The ornamental grass *Isolepis cernua* (sometimes called *Scirpus*) is a pert little number with threadlike leaves in a tuft. Water every three weeks to keep in top condition. It looks cool in a modern metallic container.

Succulents work well in this environment, too. Partridge-breasted aloe (*Aloe variegata*) makes a striking display and is a good low-maintenance choice.

Top far right Strong and beautifully shaped, the imposing fiddle-leaf fig makes a strong impact against a sandblasted brick wall.

Bottom far right The bold and sturdy foliage of this dracaena adjacent to spiky mother-in-law's tongues creates a fascinating contrast.

Middle far right The dark metallic bloom of this bat flower lends a contemporary edge to the grouping.

Right The proliferation of color in the paintings and carvings gives the indoor gardener freedom to use a myriad of pots and plants.

LIVING WITH
MODERN ART

A work of art makes its own definite statement in a room and any indoor plant has to have its own strong personality to compete for attention.

Whether the art is Renaissance, Impressionist, a framed modern print or poster, a bronze sculpture, or a tribal piece, the work is really the catalyst for the type of plant to suit the room. You can be inspired by a color or a shape in a work of art. Try to reflect that design element in the plant that you choose.

Some plants are brilliant "biosculptures" and fit into an art-filled room with ease. For an urban jungle scene like this one (right), choose plants that echo the shapes in the tribal carvings. The largest plant here is the magnificent fiddle-leaf fig (*Ficus lyrata*). The mother-in-law's tongue (*Sansevieria trifasciata* 'Laurentii') has fierce, swordlike leaves, while the begonias (rex-cultorum types) have great patterned foliage and add to the jungle feel. These are all easily available, familiar plants, given a fresh look by the setting and the containers. More unusual is the metallic-colored bat flower plant (*Tacca chantrierei*), which adds a hip urban look to a loft-style environment.

A vibrant canvas that dominates a room requires a lush plant with a comparably vibrant-colored flower; a room with a collection of smaller, Impressionist-style paintings, on the other hand, might call for a group of smaller plants, perhaps planted in traditional ceramic jardinières. Contemporary prints and posters may suit eye-catching, spiky plants with boldly variegated foliage and lots of small but elegant colored flowers.

The riot of color in the paintings in the room shown at right is repeated in the brightly patterned containers, which have been hand-painted to complement the artworks (see pages 106–7 for advice on painting pots). This is a fun, relaxed plant collection, with the accent very much on bold, tough foliage.

Note: Always use saucers under containers to protect the floor surface. Use deep saucers when you are going away for a few days since they hold more water.

Top far left The foliage of a Boston fern introduces both freshness and softness in this subtle, restrained interior.

Bottom far left Standing sentinel by the French doors in a stylish container is a bold and exotic dracaena.

Middle far left The fiery ornamental fruits of chili peppers (*Capsicum annum*) make a witty design statement.

Left Pots of wonderful chili peppers in front of a winter fire are a clever way of providing color and texture.

BOLD AND
CONTEMPORARY

Modern homes can be bland, so design accessories in clever ways to create a personal look that reflects your way of life.

The move to open-plan living doesn't just produce a clean-lined interior; it also provides opportunities to make a plant display that reflects your personality. Plants come into their own when given lots of light and space, so you can have fun choosing the variety that is best for each location you have in mind.

In an interior dominated by clean lines, pale walls, and light floors, the mood is understated. Any plant has to have a similar presence – its role is to be colorful, to lift the mood, and to introduce texture. Containers should echo the smooth lines of the furniture, and in this case (left), the contemporary style of the fireplace.

Electric or acid-green foliage will lift neutrals or cool pastel hues like pale blue. Take the bright green, jagged foliage of the Boston fern (*Nephrolepsis exaltata* 'Bostoniensis'); although this gracefully drooping variety was raised in Boston over a century ago, if you place it in a classic white ceramic pot on a stylish wood table top, it will fit into a contemporary interior with ease. The fern will grow to about 3ft (1m) high and is spreading, too, so you may like to consider moving it when it is fully grown and replace it with a younger specimen.

The ornamental chili pepper (*Capsicum annum*) grows to about 12in (30cm) tall, and bears star-shaped white flowers followed by numerous fruits, usually in bright red and yellow. These are an inspired and witty choice, especially when placed in very chic, pastel-colored tubs. For the best growing conditions, place them in full light on a windowsill.

Striking and exotic, a dracaena (*Dracaena fragrans* Deremensis Group) is at home in the light and is enough of an individual not to need grouping with other plants. Avoid direct summer sun and feed once every four weeks for strong growth.

ASIAN
FUSION STYLE

From the first trade in silks and porcelain to the current popularity of Feng Shui, Asian design has long had an influence on homes in Europe and America.

The fusion of Eastern and Western style creates environments where orchids come into their own. By this, I am not referring to the almost ubiquitous white phalaenopsis, but to the richer-colored varieties now emerging that incorporate the colors of Chinese porcelain with the simple lines of traditional Japanese furnishings.

Consider resonant and dramatic orchids such as odontoglossums – some of which are scented and give off a wonderful fragrance if placed near a seating area – or oncidiums, with their delicate flowers that resemble floating angels with wings, or even *Vuylstekeara* Cambria 'Plush', with its intricately detailed flowers. The vibrancy of these orchids chimes perfectly with the rich colors we commonly associate with the East and contrasts with the cooler tones of Western interiors.

Orchids have much to recommend them as flowering houseplants, since they flower for anywhere up to eight weeks. Furthermore, orchids are low-maintenance and require watering no more than once or twice a week. The secret to keeping your orchids healthy is to make sure that they never sit in water and to drain off any excess immediately to allow oxygen to get to their roots. Most orchids are long-lived plants that continue to flower year after year if properly cared for.

Displaying orchids in lacquered or crackle-glazed containers is usually very effective: it makes them look more opulent while at the same time suits the Eastern theme. Another way to enhance the look is with the use of clean, strong, green plants like bamboo and grasses such as *Isolepis cernua*. The small indoor bamboo (*Pogonatherum saccharoideum*) in a bamboo bowl (see far right) is a very successful combination, but for height and a more architectural statement tall bamboo plants could be used, which can be further brought to life by spotlighting (see pages 110–17).

Top far left A grouping of individual lavender plants in flower, interspersed with small buckets of shells.

Middle far left Shells evoke summer days past, either used as a decorative trim or just simply displayed in baskets or containers.

Bottom far left This echeveria has been planted in a tall tin pot and decorated with twigs topped by tiny shells.

Left A cluster of silvery-leaved succulents brings a lived-in look to a beach house; stone and shell trims were found on the seashore.

BACK TO
NATURE

Stone, smooth pebbles, shells, and driftwood are desirable elements when creating an environment far away from hard-edged industrialization.

Creating a natural look inside with plants means applying simple criteria to your plant choices. Does it look as if it could have been transplanted from outside? Are its foliage and flowers soft and colorful in a country style? Is it low-maintenance? The choice of plants is wide-ranging, from alpine succulents to cottage garden varieties. For delicacy you can't go wrong with the aptly named falling stars or Italian bellflower (*Campanula isophylla*), trailing its delicate lilac, blue, or white flowers from small, pale-green foliage.

Fragrance is an important part of this concept and another delicate-looking plant, lavender (*Lavandula*), will provide this as long as it is given lots of light and is fed and watered regularly. What could be more natural?

Flaming Katy (*Kalanchoe*) is a compact, shrublike succulent with interesting leaves; it produces dense flower heads from winter through to summer. Another favorite

succulent is the pretty echeveria (*Echeverea secunda* var. *glauca* 'Gigantea'). Stems of red and yellow flowers strike out of rosettes of divine blue-gray fleshy leaves in early summer, making the plant a conversation piece.

Seasonal color is another point to consider if you want to create a natural effect. In winter, choose foliage that shines, and in spring go for masses of small flowers to bring a touch of sunshine inside.

The surfaces of pots and containers are key to a successful natural look. Tin containers with a weathered country patina, stone pottery pitchers, rustic baskets, old terracotta pots decorated with sea shells or hand-painted in quiet, calm colors are the answer. Choose a pot that is in proportion with the size of the plant for the best visual effect. Try to combine a soft-looking plant with a pot that has a softer finish. Avoid highly finished pots – they are simply not natural.

Top far right Like a platoon of soldiers, this collection of desert cacti stand at attention following the line of a dividing wall.

Bottom far right Use a heavy pot for tall cacti and succulents, so they don't overbalance. A trim of stone chips adds further weight.

Middle far right Cactus spines emerge from areoles. These are also the points from which new stems and flowers are produced.

Right Lofty modern rooms and large succulents are made for each other. Here, a tall euphorbia is partnered by a younger specimen.

INSPIRED BY
ARCHITECTURE

Architects like to push the limits of domestic construction and are a continuing positive influence on the way we use room space.

Space is the ultimate luxury today, and when architect-designed, it is maximized. In an open-plan interior like this, where there are few walls, a row of strong plants can help to define zones by acting as room dividers.

Cool, clean lines set the design agenda and enable the living spaces to be galleries for sculptural plants worthy of singular attention. For urban chic, go no further than eye-catching cacti. A valuable design feature and a living sculpture, cacti are also low-maintenance. Their solid green forms are shown off to best advantage when positioned against a clean white backdrop. They are survivors, virtually indestructible, and can get by on little water. For best results, however, regular watering (once every week or two) and feeding in summer (to encourage flowers) is advisable. Try to keep the collar of the plant dry.

It's worth investing in a tall specimen for sensational impact. Be sure to buy an appropriate pot, too – tall plants

ought to live in containers chosen in proportion to the plant. Think big, bold, and simple. Natural textures are best for these plants; anything too decorative or ornate is overshadowed by the plant itself.

Take care where you place cacti – if they have spines (these grow directly from the stem and can be sharp), they can give a painful prick if brushed against or touched.

There is a black succulent, *Aeonium*, which looks fantastic in hard-edged environments. Add to the look by placing it in a smooth concrete container, making sure it has good drainage (see pages 120–21).

Cacti and succulents prefer sunshine all year for growth, yet in winter, when they are almost dormant, they like it cooler and do not need as much watering – if the plant is in a heated room, water it about once a month. They do not require feeding during the winter.

Top far left Olive trees are instant reminders of summers spent in the Mediterranean – or Florida, Israel, and other olive-growing lands.

Bottom far left Bougainvillea flowers themselves are inconspicuous but are surrounded by brilliantly colored bracts.

Middle far left Terracotta is perfect for this style – look for old, weathered specimens in flea markets and antique shops.

Left Citrus and olive trees and bougainvillea sit happily by French windows, ready to step outside in warm weather.

MODERN
MEDITERRANEAN

The undeniable charm of sun-baked Mediterranean countries is frequently recreated in interiors throughout the world.

One of the most striking features of the Mediterranean landscape is the luscious bright pink or deep purple tracts of bougainvillea climbing and tumbling over whitewashed walls in their rush to sunbathe. Commonly known as the paper flower, its blooms are see-through; its stems are woody and spiky. *Bougainvillea glabra* is the basic species, but its hybrids, such as *B.* 'Alexander', which puts on a brilliant crimson display through summer to autumn, are more widely grown.

Try combining bougainvillea with hibiscus (*Hibiscus rosa-sinensis*) for its brightly colored, magnificent trumpetlike flowers that last just a day or so. Lavish tender loving care on one and it can flower from spring to late summer (see pages 120–29 for care and maintenance). Trim it back from time to time if it threatens to get out of hand. For a reliable winter and spring sideshow, add pots of German primrose (*Primula obconica*) in a similar tone of pink or a contrasting white. Place in bright sun and do not overwater.

Choose plants that enjoy warmth and light, such as the olive (*Olea europea*), or calamondin (*Citrus mitis*), or the round kumquat (*Fortunella japonica*). At ground level, try Jerusalem cherry (*Solanum pseudocapiscum*), with its autumn and winter fruits that are effective imitation oranges (don't be tempted to eat them, since they are poisonous). For scent as well as show, choose a small lemon tree, or scented-leaved geranium (*Pelargonium* 'Fragrans') or the bushy, lemon-scented rose geranium, *Pelargonium* 'Graveolens'. A row of these on a sunny windowsill will remind you of lazy days spent in the Mediterranean. The rising heat will release their essential oils.

To set the mood, non-plant elements are essential – terracotta pots, as long as they are distressed, reclaimed, or recycled and have an interesting patina, created by salts leaching through the material. Mosaic-decorated pots work well, too. Keep away from the glossy, just-out-of-the-garden-center finish of brand new pots.

Top far right The baked-earth hues provide a moody backdrop for this variegated croton.

Bottom far right Juxtaposing plants with contrasting foliage ensures a strong look.

Middle far right African textiles in warm tones add to the safari look. Take full advantage of your trips abroad to add to your collection.

Right A striking zebra plant and a philodendron trained on a moss pole are the finishing touches that bring this African-style setting to life for me.

AFRICAN
SAFARI STYLE

Tribal masks, multi-colored textiles, and animal-skin prints are all part of a design trend that is firmly established in Western design vernacular.

Having spent my adolescence in West Africa, it gives me great pleasure to see these plants add the defining touch to an African-influenced interior. For me, Africa is about deep, burnt colors and rough textures, and this theme demands plants that create visual surprises at every turn in a room.

This selection of houseplants could be considered kitsch in another location, but they are absolutely appropriate for my African-style setting. The aptly named compact zebra plant (*Aphelandra squarrosa* 'Dania'), with its ivory-veined green leaves, is dramatic against evocative dark African wood, especially when its fantastic bright yellow flowers burst onto the scene. It is greedy, soaking up water when in a growth cycle, but needing little when it is dormant, and persnickety – it dislikes drafts and too much sun.

The sensational blushing philodendron (*Philodendron erubescens* 'Red Emerald') is a glossy-leaved, vigorous climber originally from the rainforest. Its height and presence give it enormous visual impact and, because of its size, it requires good support. Even more vibrant is the gleaming, almost leathery foliage of the tropical croton (*Codiaeum variegatum*) which has red, orange, purple, yellow, and green veins on its shiny leaves. It prefers a warm, humid environment but can be vulnerable to pests such as spider mite and scale (see page 128).

Choose either beaten copper or sturdy patterned stone and ceramic containers for these large, exotic plants. Dark colors work best when the plant itself is dramatic. With tall plants, consider the weight of the container, since this needs to balance that of the plant. For compact plants, a simple style that allows the plant to take center stage is best.

To clean glossy leaves, wipe carefully with a soft damp cloth or cotton balls. Soft new leaves should be left alone until they are firm, since they damage easily.

Top far left The jewel-like berries of the bead plant are echoed in the colorful and shimmering beaded pot covers.

Bottom far left The arching umbrella effect of this cyperus, with its long grassy leaves, provides an exotic touch.

Middle far left Metallic elements are at the heart of this style; match their shine with glossy leaves and jewel-bright flowers.

Left The exotic shape of the scutellaria's red blooms suit the warm, rich mood a Moroccan look demands.

THE ROAD TO
MOROCCO

From beaten copper, colorful textiles, and embroidered silk slippers to decorative brass ornaments, the design influence of this North African country is eternal.

To capture the feel of a sensual Moroccan-style interior, the ideal planting plan should feature lush foliage spiked with colorful flowers. Plants like this scutellaria (*Scutellaria costaricana*) add a touch of authentic spiciness – its small clusters of deep orange-red flowers burst through deep green foliage and are fabulous against a red-ochre wall, or on a tiled floor. Plants that create a heady, almost seductive atmosphere best reflect the style.

Consider exotic plants that reflect the sensuality in a North African-style room. Plants with glossy foliage and small vibrantly colored flowers are evocative of Moroccan finery. Lushness comes with plants like the rush, *Cyperus involucratus*, also known as the umbrella plant, which adds texture with its glamorous, arching foliage. Its elegant straight stems grow to about 24in (60cm) high, and are topped with a burst of smaller fluffy leaves. For a shorter variety, try the selected form 'Gracilis' at no more than 12in (30cm) tall.

The great things about these plants is they are hard to kill. You cannot over-water them. They like bright light and regular warmth, but are hardy and quite able to survive cool winters if necessary.

More exotic enhancement is provided by the gorgeous beadlike fruits on the bead plant (*Nertera granadensis*). Its dense mat of springy, creeping green leaves is covered in a mass of tiny orange berries, as small as *petit pois*. It puts on a great show during its late summer season of a few months. You may want to replace it when its red berries wither, since it is hard to coax back into bloom.

Favorite North African colors include turquoise, cobalt blue (believed to ward off spirits), and yellow, so choose containers in these colors. Brass and gold are also typical, so look for pots with lots of luster. Mosaic patterns are ideal for decorative containers, or try winding strings of colored beads around plant pots.

Top far left Scented plants make a good alternative to cut flowers. Here I used a grouping of gardenia and jasmine in small pots.

Middle far left Fragrant roses displayed adjacent to lily-of-the-valley create a scented corner in the room.

Bottom far left Bridal wreath can make a romantic centerpiece on a console in an entrance hall, producing a welcoming fragrance.

Left Groupings of delicate flowers, like these lily-of-the-valley and roses, complement soft, light-colored schemes.

THE NEW
ROMANTICS

Romance has been part of the design vocabulary since we discovered softness, comfort, color, and sensual textures are seductive.

Fragrance is a key element in creating a romantic mood, and roses, with their potent sentimental associations, are a natural choice. Choose full-bloomed varieties with larger flower-heads in soft colors for impact. Believe it or not, roses (*Rosa*) are often easier to care for than you might think. Make sure that you deadhead when see you signs of brown on the petals (see page 128).

Lily-of-the-valley (*Convallaria majalis*) has delicate white, bell-shaped flowers that produce a sweet, heavy fragrance. I love them in miniature cream-colored containers, grouped together, when they simply ooze sophistication with their hypnotic scent. In France, they are highly prized – on May 1, it is traditional to send them to loved ones as a token of affection. Although they are seasonal and only last a few weeks, their scent is not to be missed.

The gardenia (*Gardenia jasminoides*) is possessed of a sublime perfume and is a fantastic choice, combining luxuriance with fragrance. But it is temperamental and needs watering carefully with soft water (see pages 122–23). Sporting dark green leaves year-round, it produces superb waxy white flowers in summer.

Jasmine (*Jasminum polyanthum*), with its wispy shoots, also has a divine fragrance and sets a romantic tone, as does floradora (*Stephanotis floribunda*). This twines into a wreath shape with training and pruning, and produces waxy white flowers whose fragrance fills the room and lifts the spirit.

Pots and containers should echo the romantic theme: china jardinières with interesting decorative designs are ideal, as is any pot with a smooth surface finish. Pale colors are best – cream, white, pink, lilac, or blue – although as an alternative you could substitute a modern container with a glossy black finish that would provide a stronger contrast to exotic-looking blooms.

Top far left Tall umbrella grass in a stylish metallic container echoes the line of the pillar in this modern loft, yet softens its stark textures.

Bottom far left The peace lily needs light when flowering, so I move it near a window on a clear winter's day. It should not sit in full sun.

Middle far left Temper the sharpness of the agave by putting moss on top of the soil in the pot (and spray with water from time to time to keep it green).

Left A feathery grass is positioned next to a spiky agave in shiny metal containers on a polished wood floor for a striking, high-tech effect.

STYLISH
STATEMENTS

High-tech homes, where there is a fusion of the latest materials and cutting-edge design, call for smart plant choices.

Modern, clean-lined interiors can act as a gallery and are a good place to show off plants with star quality – those with large, bold leaves and thick, sculptural foliage. For a really unusual effect, the Mexican elephant's foot or pony tail (*Beaucarnea recurvata*) is impressive and low-maintenance. It has a wide stem and a wild-looking topknot of arching leaves (hence the common name). It requires a large and deep container to suit its woody, bulbous base. Like the African fiddle-leaf fig (*Ficus lyrata*), with its boldly veined glossy leaves, and elephant's ear (*Alocasia x amazonica*), with its dramatic white-veined, dark green foliage, it is also a good choice for a contemporary space.

Similarly attention-grabbing is the umbrella plant (*Cyperus albostriatus*), with reedy stems and drooping, threadlike leaves that waft in the air, bringing movement and a sense of life to the room; these grow from 8in (20cm) to 8ft (2.5m) tall. This is a plant that likes to have its feet in water, so make sure that it never dries out.

Or opt for tall pennisetum, which is a graceful type of ornamental grass. Although not a conventional houseplant, it works when you have floor-to-ceiling windows which provide it with the optimum light it needs. Pennisetum prefers its roots permanently wet and benefits from spraying with a mist of water where the air is dry (for instance, in an air-conditioned or centraly heated room). Combine pennisetum with the silvery gray tones of the architectural *Agave americana* and you have an exceptional double act.

Grouping definite forms around an expanse of floor-to-ceiling windows adds another visual dimension, walls are dissolved, and the outside appears to merge with the interior. When the weather warms up in summer, the plants could step outside (provided the pots are weather-proof), and effectively become dual-purpose decorations. Remember to bring them inside again if the temperature plummets at night.

Top far right Glazed ceramic containers are great for complementing the kalanchoe's small but charming retro flowers.

Bottom far right Place trailing spider plants against acrylic mirror wall bubbles and create instant plant chic.

Middle far right Funky 1970s glazed pots are ideal for plants with glossy leaves.

Right Houseplants are the essential touch if you want to recreate that authentic 1970s vibe.

HOUSEPLANT
REVIVAL

Plants that were popular when flared pants and acrylic furniture were in style are making a showy comeback, with help from the retro movement.

Retro style is bold and imaginative, often achieved with vibrant color and strong lines. Not for the faint-hearted, some of the retro plants have flowers in shades of red, bright yellow, and acid-orange, with, of course, the deep green of the foliage.

Pots of Kalanchoe (flaming Katy) are perfect retro plants, bringing with them a sense of 1970s style that some of us might like to forget (along with bell-bottoms and tank tops), but for a younger generation it is new and uncharted territory. These flowering succulents (usually unnamed hybrids, with red, white, yellow, or pink flowers) are great for people who are away from home a lot because they don't need a lot of watering and tolerate a certain amount of benign neglect. These plants can grow to about 12in (30cm) tall, and will flower for months on end. Look also at its close relative, Kalanchoe daigremontiana (the Devil's backbone), which can grow up to 36in (90cm) and has an abundance of fringed leaves. These plants used in groupings are a great way to achieve a chic designer look on the cheap.

On a larger scale, the delightfully familiar *Monstera deliciosa* (known as the Swiss cheese plant because of its holed, glossy leaves) is at home in any corner as long as it has the support of a bamboo cane or something similar.

The return of pert plastic and acrylic furniture also opens up a window of opportunity for cute plants such as the spider plant, *Chlorophytum comosum* 'Vittatum', with its cascading stems and tiny white flowers. It is a low-maintenance plant, though too much heat and not enough light will leave it looking pale and wan. Its partner in style-crime is *Crassula ovata*, known as the jade plant. The Chinese, following a Feng Shui tradition, put it in the window to entice good fortune, hence it is also called the money plant. Both of these need a splash of water from time to time, and in winter make sure that they do not dry out.

COLOR

SCENT

CHOOSING
SCENTED PLANTS

Scented rooms have an invaluable place in our sensory vocabulary, reminding us of magical moments, revived when we encounter a similar aroma.

Throughout our lives we all build up a memory bank of fragrant associations, and it is to your personal "library" of scents that you should turn when deciding which houseplants will be perfect in a room.

When deciding where to place a fragrant plant, look at the seating area. It would be a shame to place it away from where you sit most of the time. Sitting it on a table adjacent to a sofa is perfect for enjoying the fragrance at close quarters, so is a table that you pass several times a day, since you get to smell the fragrance on each occasion.

Each plant has a signature fragrance, and for it to be fully appreciated it requires space. Placing two or three competing fragrances together is detrimental to the power of each and confuses the senses.

Also, consider the size of the room. Plants with a powerful fragrance are overwhelming in a small room, while in a large traditional living room or modern loft space you may find that you need several containers of the same plant placed around the room to really appreciate their scent.

FRESH SCENTS

Plants that produce refreshing, uplifting aromas that add a fresh note are easy to grow in the right conditions. The following plants are worth considering:

● In the kitchen: sweet basil (*Ocimum basilicum*) – rub the leaves together for an instant fragrance hit. Lemon-scented thyme (*Thymus x citriodorus* 'Aureus') is bushy, with fresh lemon-scented, golden-green leaves. A mint bush (*Prostanthera rotundifolia*) – each time you brush by it, a minty aroma is released from its leaves.
● Some pelargoniums are well-known for their scented leaves. Try, for instance, *P.* 'Fragrans', *P.* 'Lady Plymouth', or *P.* 'Old Spice'.
● Narcissi – tazetta narcissi (*Narcissus* hybrids) have beautiful cream flowers in late autumn through to spring, and like a warm place in the sun. Use these to bring a sense of early spring inside.

HEADY SCENTS

Rich scents always promote a sense of well-being. Indulge your senses with some of the following heady houseplants:
● Hyacinths (*Hyacinthus orientalis* hybrids) are glorious. Their distinct fragrance is superb in late winter and spring.
● Gardenias (*Gardenia augusta* cultivars) are showy plants with large, double creamy white flowers in summer and autumn, and give off a divine exotic fragrance.
● Easter lilies (*Lilium longiflorum*) grow to 36in (90cm) and produce very fragrant trumpet-shaped flowers in warm and moderately humid conditions.
● Miniature irises (*Iris reticulata*) grow to 6in (15cm) high and bear fragrant flowers in late winter.

Top right The rich golden hue of sweet-smelling tazetta narcissi.

Top far right A small citrus produces delightful fresh scents, and fruit for a gin and tonic without even moving outside.

Bottom right The waxy blooms of the gardenia are richly fragrant.

Bottom far right Tubular bells of a floradora about to burst open.

Other fragrant plants
Lily-of-the-valley *Convallaria majalis*
Grape hyacinth *Muscari armeniacum*
Rosemary *Rosmarinus officinalis*
Chocolate plant *Cosmos atrosanguineus*
Odontoglossum *Odontoglossum hybrids*
Jasmine *Jasminum polyanthum*

MAKING
COLOR CHOICES

Creating the ambience in a room requires an understanding of how color influences moods. With houseplants, we can use nature as the inspiration.

Color stimulates the creative senses, and can provide enormous emotional satisfaction. Looking at the sunlight filtering through a delicate tulip petal can be a breathtaking experience that will remain locked in your memory for ever. Personality affects color preferences. To some people, only a brilliant red can satisfy, bringing vibrancy and vitality to a color scheme; to others the palest shade of cream is perfect. It is important to work out the colors to which you are instinctively drawn, and those about which you are ambivalent.

MATCHING COLORS

Observe how nature matches colors – it combines foliage, which ranges in color from green through to silvery gray, with white, yellow (the buttercup being the brightest example), orange, red, blue, purple, lilac – right through the color chart. Here are just a few examples of nature's talent for matching colors:

● White, cream, and a hint of palest yellow. These are "cool" colors, which when grouped together create a sophisticated effect in any setting. They have a purity that is peaceful, almost spiritual, matched by no other color in the spectrum.

● Blue, pale blue, and a hint of lilac. Each of these colors is from a similar segment of the spectrum and flowers in any of these shades will produce a calming effect when displayed together.

● Red, pink, and a hint of pale orange. Warm colors within the same "family" have an inviting ambience that brings vitality into a plant selection.

● Yellow and gold. Strong colors such as these have a powerful impact in a room, and can look fabulous when plants are grouped en masse.

● Green. The basic color of all plant leaves, this always has a calming effect. Mix different shades together to create a rich but restful picture.

CLASHING COLORS

Some colors shout out loud when combined, giving the senses a disturbing jolt. The following are some examples of what not to put together:

● Red and blue flowers. The red will detract from the vibrancy of the deep blue and vice versa. Each is bold and beautiful in its own right; there is no need to mix them. Purple flowers are also best kept away from red and blue.

● Yellow and deep purpley black flowers as seen in some of the more innovatively bred tulips. The sight of the two together offends almost immediately.

● Purple and orange flowering plants. Vibrant colors, yes, but one will fight the other for attention if they are placed near each other.

Again, the rules for combining color are personal, and what I think clashes may look like heaven to you. Common sense generally prevails.

Top right The elegant white flower of the luscious peace lily.

Top far right For sheer beauty, look no further than the delicate flowers of an orchid.

Bottom right The pale variegated foliage of a dieffenbachia is striking.

Bottom far right The florists' classic, cyclamen is still my favorite, despite the trend for more extraordinary plants.

Wonderful whites
Begonia *Begonia x tuberhybrida* (white varieties)
Paper flower *Bougainvillea* (white varieties)
Citrus *Citrus*
Lily-of-the-valley *Convallaria majalis*
Gardenia *Gardenia augusta*
Hyacinth *Hyacinthus orientalis* (white varieties)

Pretty pinks

Begonia *Begonia x tuberhybrida*
  (pink varieties)
Paper flower *Bougainvillea*
  (pink varieties)
Cyclamen *Cyclamen persicum*
  (pink varieties)
Amaryllis *Hippeastrum*
  (pink varieties)
Hyacinths *Hyacinthus orientalis*
  (pink varieties)
Hydrangea *Hydrangea*
  macrophylla

Bottom far left Pretty in pink – the waxy bloom on the leaves of this succulent echeveria have a pronounced rosy tinge.
.

Bottom left The delicately fragrant, tubular flowers of tropical bouvardias are carried in dainty, posylike clusters.

Bottom right This tillandsia, a bromeliad from the Peruvian Amazon, has intriguing, shrimp-pink flowers.

Bottom far right The beautifully marked, pewter-gray leaves of this urn plant are the perfect foil to the luminous pink flowers.

Left The brilliant green fronds of an upright Boston fern.

Top right Crowns of delicate, feathery leaves top the reedlike stems of the umbrella plant.

Top far right Standing proud, the leathery leaves of the mother-in-law's tongue are boldly edged with yellow and banded with zebralike stripes.

Bottom right The silvery green leaves of this succulent aloe have distinctive toothed edges.

Bottom far right The maidenhair fern is a mass of soft green foliage.

Gorgeous greens

Bird's nest fern *Asplenium nidus*
Hard fern *Blechnum* species
Tree ivy *Fatshedera lizei*
Weeping fig *Ficus benjamina*
Kentia palm *Howea fosteriana*
Isolepis cernua
Swiss cheese plant *Monstera deliciosa*
Blushing philodendron *Philodendron erubescens*

Far left Leaves in addition to flowers can provide color. The spiny, fleshy, glaucous blue leaves of this aloe are a long-term attraction, perfectly offset by the granite chips.

Top left Hyacinths have a powerful scent that matches the depths of their colors – in this case, a rich purplish blue.

Bottom left This hydrangea has flowers of an intense electric blue, offset by white centers.

Beautiful blues
Campanula carpatica
Falling stars *Campanula isophylla*
Echeveria **species**
Bluebell *Hyacinthoides non-scripta*
Lavender *Lavandula*
Rosemary *Rosmarinus officinalis*
African violet *Saintpaulia*

COLOR SCHEMES

The color scheme of a room also has a bearing on the colors you decide upon for houseplants. Good advice from experts is to start with a favorite color and choose a group of similar hues that work with it. Experiment with smaller, inexpensive plants first, before making that exuberantly colorful choice. A living room with white walls and pale flooring cries out for a splash of color — sometimes not present even in the furniture and soft furnishings. In such a scheme, an interesting tall, elegant plant with exotic foliage and a shot of color in its blooms can add enormous impact. As can a group of smaller plants in one color — perhaps four or five pots of purple hyacinths on a tray in the middle of the table.

FOLIAGE COLOR

Colorful foliage, too, is impressive in its own quiet way. There are quite a few choices: purple and white, almost black, variegated green and yellow, subtle shades of green (as seen in the ubiquitous maidenhair fern, page 43) and that gorgeous silvery gray with red of the ornamental cabbage (right). Some foliage is magically in two shades, the top of the leaf being one shade, the underside in another shade entirely, for instance the peacock plant (*Stromanthe* 'Stripestar'), which has a dark green leaf decorated by a pale green midrib, and a dark purple underside.

Top far left The African violet used to be thought of as an old lady's plant, but the younger generation should also consider its charms.

Bottom far left The closest to a "black" plant, the ophiopogon has leaves that are always a conversation piece.

Top left All rex begonias have brilliant leaves, with a pronounced metallic sheen. The flowers are inconspicuous and can be removed if you wish.

Bottom left Ornamental cabbages produce their best colors as the temperature dips in winter – but don't eat them!

Deep purples

Elephant's ear plant *Alocasia sanderiana*
Chili pepper *Capsicum annuum*
Cyclamen *Cyclamen persicum* hybrids
Hyacinth *Hyacinthus orientalis* hybrids
Moth orchid *Phalaenopsis* hybrids
German primrose *Primula obconica*
Tradescantia pallida 'Purpurea'
Wandering Jew *Tradescantia zebrina* 'Purpusii'

Radical reds

Begonia *Begonia x tuberhybrida*
  (red varieties)
Paper flower *Bougainvillea* (red
  varieties)
Desert cacti (some species)
Chili pepper *Capsicum annuum*
Cyclamen *Cyclamen persicum*
  (red varieties)
Rose of China *Hibiscus rosa-
  sinensis* (red varieties)
Amaryllis *Hippeastrum* (red
  varieties)
Flaming Katy *Kalanchoe*
Medinilla magnifica

Bottom far left At home in tropical Africa, gerberas have lipstick-red daisy-like flowers of unmatched vibrancy. Use them as the centerpiece of any grouping of plants.

Bottom left Not actually flowers – which are inconspicuous – the terminal bracts produced by the guzmania are as brilliant as any blossom.

Bottom right Scutellarias seem to have burst into flame when the intense scarlet flowers appear during summer.

Bottom far right You can hardly fail with clivias, one of the easiest of all flowering houseplants to grow. The vibrant orange and yellow flowers are reliably produced each spring.

Far left All crotons have dramatically marked foliage. This is the appropriately named 'Gold Star', which has leaves generously streaked and mottled with yellow.

Top left Tuberous begonias have flowers that can easily be mistaken for roses, as this rich golden-yellow variety amply demonstrates.

Bottom left Most kalanchoes have red or pink flowers, but recent breeding programs have extended the color range to include a brilliant yellow as illustrated here.

Mellow yellows

Zebra plant *Aphelandra squarrosa*
Desert cacti (some species)
Chili pepper *Capsicum annuum*
Dracaena fragrans **Deremensis Group**
Transvaal daisy *Gerbera jamesonii* **hybrids**
Jerusalem cherry *Solanum pseudocapsicum*

SHAPE

PATTERN

TEXTURE

PLANT
PROPORTIONS

The question of size is paramount for both plant and container. One element must balance the other for harmony to be achieved.

The proportions of the room in which your chosen plant will be living are also a consideration. In a large room with high ceilings choose a tall plant with a real presence – nothing too spindly, but something exotic, such as the magnificent aloe (*Aloe vera*), which is a great personal favorite of mine, illustrated on the opposite page. Its strong, almost aggressive form and its dangerous-looking fleshy, textural leaves dictate the type of territory it requires: masses of space. Large plants emphasize the space in which they live; smaller plants provide a small-scale theatrical dimension. There are no rules other than keeping a sense of proportion.

PLACES FOR TALL PLANTS

The best places for tall plants are those which will benefit from the addition of a focal point. The more physical interest there is on a tall plant, the more it will need a platform for its splendor.

● A plain painted wall or a wood-paneled wall at the end of a medium- to large-sized room makes a great backdrop for tall, spiky plants whose foliage will stand out against the textural surface.

● Use tall plants as a room divider to hide a home office in the corner of a living room, or an exercycle area in a bedroom. Leafy plants give best coverage.

● For impact in an entrance hall, place a specimen plant in a medium-lit corner.

● Set a group of several tall plants against large picture windows for good effect – they can even act as a privacy screen, obviating the need for curtains.

PLACES FOR SMALL PLANTS

Anywhere that cries out for a spot of color or texture is good for small plants. For greater impact, group them in two's or three's, whether on a kitchen bench, tabletop, or the floor.

● If you want to display one sensational plant on a bedside table, choose a small one that won't easily be knocked over, and place it on the side furthest from the bed, so that it has room to grow out.

● Plants placed on the end of bookshelves can ramble and cascade down to the next shelf or beyond.

● In a small room, a luscious yet low-growing flowering plant on a side table adds elegance.

● Corners and hard-edged flat surfaces benefit from the softening effect of miniature ferns.

● Put one or two exotic little plants that like humidity on a steamy bathroom shelf or windowsill.

PLACES FOR COMPACT PLANTS

Small cacti are the most interesting compact plants, closely followed by other succulents of the aloe variety.

● Place several identical low-growing plants on a coffee table (with attractive saucers under each plant).

Right The patina on this slate pot is a perfect complement to the mat aloe leaves. Placing three of these in a row in an open-plan room was a stroke of genius.

Tall plants
Dieffenbachia sanguine 'Exotica'
Euphorbia abyssinica
Weeping fig *Ficus benjamina*
Amaryllis *Hippeastrum* hybrids
Kentia palm *Howea fosteriana*
Swiss cheese plant *Monstera deliciosa*

Small plants
Desert cacti (young plants)
Falling stars *Campanula isophylla*
Cyclamen *Cyclamen persicum* hybrids
Flaming Katy *Kalanchoe* hybrids

• Put a group on a windowsill in any room. If it's in full sun, put them in the shade for the hottest period of the day and water as required.

PLACES FOR SPREADING PLANTS

Specimens that spread need lots of space around them, either so they don't get brushed as you walk by, causing damage, or so that their foliage doesn't become entangled with the plant next door. Climbers need things they can get their hooks into; trailers need wide open spaces to meander along.

• Center stage on a mantelpiece or in an open display cabinet is a convenient spot for strong, broad-leaved foliage plants.

• A long ledge under a window, or above a bookshelf, is good for flowering plants with lots of foliage.

When choosing a container for any of these sizes, remember this golden rule: the plant should measure about one third of the final combination; two thirds is taken up by the container. Also, try to imagine how large the plant is going to grow — will it "grow into" its pot after a few weeks? If you don't want to look at the soil until it's covered by foliage, cover it with small white pebbles or even soft and sexy moss. This also helps to keep moisture in during the important early days.

Top far left This guzmania spreads as wide as it is tall, so site it where you can be sure you won't brush against it in passing.

Bottom far left These young barrel cacti, grouped together for maximum impact, are squat, compact plants that won't fall over easily – low-maintenance too!

Top left Slipper orchids are tall, elegant plants best seen in splendid isolation. Staking ensures that the slender flower stem won't keel over.

Bottom left Play with scale. Setting this diminutive rat's-tail cactus in an over-large planter lessens the chances of you catching your hands on its spines.

Compact plants
Aloe aristata
Partridge-breasted aloe *Aloe variegata*
Desert cacti (young plants)
Echeveria species
African violets *Saintpaulia* hybrids

Spreading plants
Urn plant *Aechmea fasciata*
Spider plant *Chlorophytum comosum* 'Vittatum'
Kentia palm *Howea fosteriana*
Medinilla magnifica
Boston fern *Nephrolepis exaltata* 'Bostoniensis'

EXPLOITING
LEAF SHAPE

When a plant has extraordinary foliage it is a good long-term investment, since it will be a fabulous focal point throughout the year.

Dramatic effects can be achieved with foliage. The bigger and more extraordinarily shaped, the stronger the visual reaction. What is it about plants with great foliage that attracts us? For one thing, they emphasize the underlying philosophy that plants are an integral part of a room's design, not a last-minute addition to fill an empty space. They have splendid architectural form, complementing the clean lines in a room. Also, leaves are enticing – you want to touch them, smell them, and they give hours of visual pleasure. They can be small, large, soft, featherlike, furry, strong, oval, round, pointed, stand to attention like sentinels or arch, swoon, or squiggle in chaotic abandonment.

Leaves range in size and shape from the tiny foliage of baby's tears (*Soleirolia soleirolii*), to the larger creeping fig (*Ficus pumila*) and pilea leaves and some of the ivies (*Hedera*) and wandering Jew (*Tradescantia*), and lastly, to those in the super-leaf league, the fiddle-leaf fig (*Ficus lyrata*), mother-in-law's tongue (*Sansevieria trifasciata* 'Laurentii'), philodendron, and Swiss cheese plant (*Monstera deliciosa*).

For unique style, houseplants with narrow or sword-shaped foliage are fantastic. They are instant conversation pieces and if used effectively can become the mainstay of a grouping on a floor or ledge. Narrow leaves add height,

starring above a display of three or four more compact plants. In design terms, tall plants with narrow leaves break up the horizontal lines that form with such a grouping. Also, vertical leaves are essential for those narrow spaces for which you despaired of ever finding a suitable plant.

Large plant leaves are not necessarily on dominating plants, for instance the dumb cane (*Dieffenbachia seguine*) grows only to about a yard, but has leaves up to 18in (45cm) long. Depending on the variety, they can be liberally splashed or edged with creamy white or yellow. The Japanese aralia (*Fatsia japonica*) also has sensationally large leaves that spread open like fans, though in a container the plant is of only modest dimensions overall. This is the ideal choice for creating a focal point against a plain wall. It will amaze, as will crystal anthurium (*Anthurium crystallinum*), which is blessed with large, dark green, velvety leaves with prominent white veins.

Small plants also have their charms. Take the string of beads (*Senecio rowleyanus*), for one, which produces a collection of tiny, beadlike leaves hanging over the edge of the pot on fine threads.

Place contrasting leaf shapes together, mixing tall and short plants with a variety of habits, i.e. some that grow vertically with others that arch elegantly, or have a spreading habit.

Top right Most grasses have long, slender leaves. Those of this isolepis are threadlike and arch over like a filament lamp.

Top far right The bird's-nest fern has bright shiny green, wavy-edged fronds that curl over at the tips.

Bottom right The leaves of the false aralia are toothed like a chain saw.

Bottom far right Like peas in a pod, the leaves of the string of beads are almost perfectly spherical.

USING PATTERN & TEXTURE

Many plants also have a tactile quality: any with textured leaves, or flowers, will complement your decor if you use them creatively.

Plants with soft, velvety foliage, broad-patterned leaves or spectacular spines will become the focal point in a room, so it's advisable to use them in a theatrical way. Choose each plant for a specific purpose: if you want to make a fashion statement on a dining table, use a low-growing cactus or another variety of succulent with striking, broad leaves. It is vital that guests can see each other across the table. Set two or three containers in a shallow, clear acrylic container, top the soil with tiny white frosty chips of stone – voila! You may like to use pots of slender club-rush (*Isolepsis cernua*) in a row, or the pretty baby's tears (*Soleirolia soleirolii* 'Variegata') with its tiny silvered leaves forming a creeping carpet. Put these in small modern terracotta or metallic pots and you will have created a chic setting.

Some plants have everything, like the golden barrel cactus (*Echinocactus grusonii*). It's a round, prickly ball and has a masculinity about it which makes it perfect for a New Man in his urban, high-tech environment. Any of the agave tribe (particularly *A. victoriae-reginae*) and some kalanchoes (such as *K. thyrsiflora*) suit this environment, too.

If you want a specimen plant for a dull corner, look for something tall, leafy, and exotic. The lush Colombian rainforest plant crystal anthurium (*Anthurium crystallinum*) has large, dark green leaves patterned with white veins.

Their surface is smooth, like velvet in appearance. It requires high humidity and to be kept moist and out of the way of any drafts.

Choose plants with sex appeal; look for leaf texture – tough and glossy deep green, soft and covered in tiny hairs, studded with dangerous spikes, and wound in fine threads, red-tipped leaves, or just wild and wilful structures such as the corkscrew rush (*Juncus effusus* 'Spiralis'), whose tendrils wriggle all over the place.

For pattern, choose plants with dramatically veined leaves in cream or pink, variegated green and yellow or green and white broad leaves, or plants with speckled, striped, and rippled leaf effects. Wandering Jew or inch plant (*Tradescantia zebrina* 'Quadricolor') grows to about 10in (25cm) and it likes to wander everywhere it can, either down from a hanging basket or along from a container on a high shelf. Its green leaves are patterned with silver stripes and a hue of pink and red is visible, too.

The trusty tiger begonia (a rex-cultorum type) is a compact plant with dark foliage dotted with splashes of yellow and is just one of many begonias with flair. The painted-leaf begonia has lop-sided leaves shaded a deep, warm pink; others put on a silvery show, or purple, purple and red, red, green and pink... oh, and plain green.

Top right The corkscrew rush – obvious how it got its name, is it not?

Top far right Touchy-feely. The smooth, pewter-gray leaves of this kalanchoe are crying out to be stroked lovingly.

Bottom right In the wild, the spiny margins of the agave keep chomping animals at bay – so handle with care.

Bottom far right The roly-poly barrel cactus is barbarously armed with thick spines, sharp as needles, that shine luminous gold in sunlight.

Top far left The kris plant has dramatic, arrow-shaped leaves with silver veining and a pronounced metallic sheen.

Top left Blissfully easy to grow and seemingly at home anywhere, the wandering Jew has peppermint-striped leaves that positively gleam.

Bottom left 'Norah Bedson' is just one of a huge number of begonias that are grown for their strikingly marked leaves.

SITES

STATEMENTS
AT THE ENTRANCE

Very often a foyer or entrance hall is a bland, uninspiring place, so it is the ideal place for the type of plants that are welcoming and will add attitude.

An entrance hall creates the first impression, it is the link between the exterior and what is to come inside. So often halls are neglected because they're considered too narrow, too dark, and, besides, you only pass through on the way to somewhere else.

Yet the hall is the vital introduction to your home, setting the style, and should be treated with respect. Architectural details are more apparent in halls, so complement these features with a clever choice of plants.

IDEAS FOR HALLWAYS

In long, narrow halls where space is at a premium, choose compact plants with impact. The choice of display areas is limited, so use them imaginatively.

● Center stage on a narrow console against the wall is perfect for foliage affairs, such as asparagus fern (*Asparagus setaceus* 'Nanus'), or plants that will bear small but gorgeous flowers or fruits, such as ornamental peppers (*Capsicum annum* 'Festival Orange').

● Choose a pot in similar colors to those on the wall or on the floor. It also should be of a medium size so it doesn't grab attention or look too big in the narrow space.

● In a more spacious area, you can be adventurous. A line of small pots acts as a trail from the front door, gently beckoning your visitors onward and through to the rest of the house.

● Choose small plants with similar growth habits that will add a welcoming and colorful touch.

● The containers are important, too, especially if you want to create a trail. They really ought to be the same size and color for a successful grouping. In the setting (left) I used small white ceramic pots that have a smooth glazed finish and are all identical. They are the perfect complement to the glossy white floor and stairs.

IDEAS FOR STAIRS

Usually, stairs are designed for practicality – moving up to another level. This often means there is not much spare space. They can be drafty, so you have to choose plants that like this situation.

● On narrow stairs with a landing halfway up, place an attractive stool or plant holder from a second-hand store. Here you can display plants with medium spread or even trailers such as string of beads (*Senecio rowleyanus*) or wandering Jew (*Tradescantia fluminensis* 'Albovittata'). If the light levels are low, a fern can fit the bill.

● Containers full of bulbs such as crocuses put on a cheerful show and can be planted in the garden after they have flowered.

● Small containers placed to one side of each stair tread look fantastic. Choose plants such as cacti, a velvet-leaved kalanchoe, or the amazing slender club-rush (*Isolepsis cernua*) for effect.

Left This sentinel line of baby's tears looks almost like a row of topiary specimens, bringing a touch of well-groomed sophistication to a simply conceived hallway.

Plants that put up with drafty places
Agave victoriae-reginae
Cast-iron plant *Aspidistra elatior*
Cacti (desert species)
Echeveria species
Weeping fig *Ficus benjamina*
Olive *Olea europea*
Mother-in-law's tongue
  Sansevieria trifasciata
  'Laurentii'

ARRANGEMENTS FOR
THE LIVING ROOM

The living room is the heart of a home, where friends are invited to relax and be entertained – and where plants are destined for display.

The decoration of your living space will determine the style demanded by the plants. The same rule applies whether it is a traditional room, an Art Deco space, or Victorian. Examine the features in your living room and take a lead from them – does one shape dominate? Is it purely color and does it need a calming plant? Are the accessories textural and so require textural foliage to complement the look? The following are just a few ideas you should consider.

IDEAS FOR FAMILIES

Plants that can withstand a lot of activity around them, and occasional neglect, are ideal. Delicate flowers such as orchids are not suitable, and soft foliage will not stand much chance of survival in a family living room with a cat, dog, and children! If you have small children, be careful where you place any plants that have sharp, pointed leaves and spiny cacti.

● For shelves and windowsills, choose ferns with arching fronds such as the Boston fern (*Nephrolepsis exaltata* 'Bostoniensis') or bromeliads, such as blushing bromeliad (*Neoregelia coralinae* f. *tricolor*) with its dense, bold, shiny green leaves. In the flowering season, it produces an eye-catching red heart.

● Trailing plants look cool when placed on high display shelves. Out of the way of small hands, they can grow to their hearts' content.

IDEAS FOR MANTELS OVER FIREPLACES

● Miniature iris (*Iris reticulata*) has fragrant flowers in late winter and grows to about 6in (15cm).

● Fleshy succulents such as aloes and echeverias will thrive in the warm, dry air above the fireplace.

● Cacti like mantels and there are a lots to choose from. Look for similar shapes, and those that will produce flowers at the same time. Line up a range of heights from the left to right, tallest to smallest. Choose stylish containers for them, since they will be prominent in the room.

● One showpiece makes a strong style statement. Choose a medium-sized plant that likes warmth and doesn't trail (no singed leaves). An amaryllis (*Hippeastrum*) is simply amazing, growing to about 20in (50cm). Its trumpet-shaped flowers burst forth in winter or spring.

IDEAS FOR OCCASIONS

● A wedding party at home requires miniature roses in tin or ceramic containers. Choose double petal varieties that will look exquisite grouped together on a table top or windowsill. 'Cinderella' has double, silvery pink petals and a whiff of fragrance.

● Parties of any kind need dressing up. Plants with bold, interestingly shaped foliage, in unusual containers are ideal. Take a large, shallow, clear plexiglass container, fill with soil, add eight hyacinths (*Hyacinthus orientalis*) and cover the soil with tiny white stone chips. Easy, chic appeal.

Right Clivias are among the easiest of houseplants to grow and will produce a show of vivid orange-red flowers every spring. The simple beauty of the arching, leathery, shiny green leaves is not to be sniffed at either, and the whole plant contributes a cool elegance to this understated interior.

Plants that purify air
Spider plant *Chlorophytum comosum* 'Vittatum'
Dumb cane *Dieffenbachia seguine*
Dracaena fragrans **Deremensis Group**
Weeping fig *Ficus benjamina*
Rubber plant *Ficus elastica*
False aralia *Schefflera elegantissima*

Left For a touch of night-time glamor, these calla lilies are unsurpassed. The golden bowl of glass chips in which they appear to be growing, together with the glass and chrome table, seem to reflect a halo of light around them.

Right By day the ensemble is equally sophisticated, but now the look is high-tech and coolly elegant.

HERBS
IN THE KITCHEN

Kitchens are generally functional places, where the greenery that indoor plants bring is especially welcome: living herbs that can be used to liven up your cooking are the supremely practical choice.

In most households – whether urban or rural – the kitchen is one of the central rooms of the house. Generally warm and well-lit, it offers the ideal environment for growing culinary herbs. Besides adding distinction to your cooking, herbs also have valuable restorative qualities – as you can discover by running your fingertips along a thyme or rosemary plant to release the powerful aromatic oils – and a cup of chamomile tea makes an excellent nightcap at the end of a stressful day.

GROWING HERBS

I prefer to buy my herbs from a garden center or nursery, as invariably supermarket-bought plants are on the spindly side, being intended to provide leaves for a few meals only. Strong-growing plants will provide leaves for much longer. Evergreens such as rosemary and bay can be used throughout winter. The green-thumbed could try growing tender herbs such as basil and parsley from seed.

● Most herbs are best in a nutrient-low, fairly gritty soil mix that drains easily, apart from mint, which appreciates a damp growing medium.

● Keep herbs on a sunny windowsill. Open the window periodically to keep the air around them moving.

● Pinching out the growing tips from time to time produces compact, bushy plants.

● Mist the plants every once in a while to keep them fresh and to release their evocative aroma.

STYLING IDEAS FOR CONTAINERS

The containers you choose should be suitable for herbs – most need good drainage – as well as reflecting the style of your kitchen.

● In a rustic kitchen, distressed terracotta pots are ideal. They can be painted to match the decor. Shallow troughs are particularly good for low-growing herbs such as thymes and marjoram.

● Galvanized metal containers suit a high-tech interior.

● For that seaside look, wooden containers can be given a wash of white paint for a weathered, salted appearance.

COOKING WITH HERBS

Most dishes are best with only one or two herbs. Some are very strong and in excess can easily overpower more delicate flavors.

● Pesto is traditionally made by crushing together basil, garlic, and pine nuts and adding olive oil and a hard cheese such as parmesan. However, you can substitute other herbs such as rosemary, parsley, or oregano, using almonds or walnuts in place of the pine nuts.

● Arugula has slightly bitter leaves that make an excellent, palate-cleansing salad, either on their own or with lettuce.

● Bay leaves are delicious in tomato-based sauces as well as in winter stews and casseroles.

● Basil, the typical Mediterranean herb, is actually from India so is essential in any Fusion dish.

Right An old metal colander used as an improvised container planted with a mixture of herbs – variegated thyme, basil, and marjoram – provides effective drainage, as well as having that pre-war, granny's kitchen look. The meat tray underneath protects the work surface from water damage but should be emptied promptly, as most herbs hate sitting with their feet in excess water.

Easy-to-grow herbs

Chives *Allium schoenoprasum*
Chamomile *Chamaemelum nobile*
Arugula *Eruca vesicaria*
Bay *Laurus nobilis*
Mint *Mentha*
Basil *Ocimum basilicum*
Marjoram *Origanum*
Parsley *Petroselinum crispum*
Rosemary *Rosmarinus officinalis*

CENTERPIECES FOR
THE DINING ROOM

A floral centerpiece is the one essential element of setting the dining table for a special occasion. Without it, the table looks unfinished.

Before choosing a plant for the table, there are several aspects to consider. The first is that the plant should not be more than 10in (25cm) high to make sure that guests can see whoever is seated on the other side. Secondly, avoid plants with too strong a fragrance as this may detract from the aroma of the various dishes served.

STYLING IDEAS

If you decide to create a lunch or dinner party with a theme, then all accessories must carry that theme through, and that includes the style of plant.

● For an oriental theme, choose small, rectangular containers in red or black with a lacquer finish, and fill with single plants such as coral moss (*Nertera granadensis*), which sprouts a dense green mat dotted with bright orange berries. Or consider the bright green mass of baby's tears (*Soleirolia soleirolii*), whose tiny mass of foliage grows to just 2in (5cm).

● Salsa food cries out for cacti. Try a row of fish-hook cacti (*Ferocatus latispinus*) – at 10in (25cm) high, they just meet the height requirements – with aggressive spikes all over their round form. Also, tiger jaws (*Faucaria tigrina*), whose succulent leaves have sharp, jagged edges; it bursts into yellow flowers in autumn.

● Formal occasions require restrained, elegant plants. Slender club-rush (*Isolepsis cernua*) will be perfect all in a row, preferably in glazed white pots.

TABLE DECORATION

Putting a plant in a container and placing it on the table require thought. Most people have a certain dinner service for the occasion. Match the flowers and their pots with the shape and colors in the dinner set and table napkins. Plain services are best. Heavily patterned ones detract from the effect of the plants.

● A white theme: add one or two fashionable platters under a white container, as shown in the photograph left. Think small. For four guests, use four individual plants and platters so they can take them home.

● Create a trailing effect: choose a trailing ivy with variegated green and silvery leaves and place one at each end of the table. Trail the ivy to the center of the table, where sit three small round candles wrapped in wide silver mesh ribbon. Weave the ivy in and around the ribbon.

● Individual miniature cream roses in rustic pots or baskets placed at each setting, tied with natural fiber bows, create a country-style ambience.

● Several small grape hyacinths (*Muscari armeniacum*) placed evenly along the table can be linked with a trail of ribbon decorated with bunches of grapes.

● Almost translucent, eerie moonstones (*Pachyphytum oviferum*) take table design out of the box and into the future. Place in small, shiny metal containers and put three close together on silver lacquered boxes at either end of the table.

Left Cyclamen are among the best flowering houseplants, with their elegant flowers and exquisitely marked foliage. Here, a variety in virginal white has been matched to a simple glazed pot set on two matching square plates of different sizes. The quiet distinction of this arrangement ceates an interesting focal point, yet will not distract attention from your delicious cooking.

SENSUAL IDEAS FOR
BEDROOMS

We spend up to a third of our lives in bed, which makes it imperative that we pay attention to the plants we place in the rest zone.

Plants in the bedroom help to create a sense of harmony, or excite, depending upon the desired ambience. The sensuality inherent in the form of a dendrobium orchid is breathtaking. These plants lend an exotic air, and many varieties are exquisitely scented. There are thousands of varieties and hybrids to choose from – look for the spare, sensual varieties such as 'Golden Shower'. The latter are best for "beginners" since they respond well to watering and feeding. Slipper orchids (*Paphiopedilum*) feature slipperlike flowers – a witty idea for a bedroom – which are produced over an eight-week period between autumn and spring. All orchids need good light, but avoid direct sunlight. A place by the window is best, especially in winter. Artificial lighting enhances flowering, so you may want to investigate the correct type to use.

Scent can overpower in a bedroom, so if you want a fragrant plant choose with care. Consider a delicately scented plant like lavender, which is renowned for its relaxing qualities. A small pot placed on a bedside table is beneficial. There are many varieties to choose from, but all will have the desired effect. It is best to avoid very heavily scented plants such as gardenias and jasmine. On a hot sultry night, the scent could well be too much.

Pelargoniums and primroses are also good choices for the bedroom – they have a wide color range, so a harmonious look is easy to achieve. For serenity, avoid cluttering surfaces with lots of small pots. One fine flower can leave a memorable impression – bear in mind that less is more, and that the most pleasure is derived from a light touch.

Colored containers can influence the mood; go for white, cream, pale blue, and soft lilac for serenity. Mat finishes, rather than gloss, are preferable for creating a calm mood.

STYLING IDEAS

Many plants will be at home in a bedroom and can be used to enhance any style you may wish to create.

● For a colonial feel, try a palm such as the majesty palm (*Ravenea rivularis*) in a basket in a corner of the room. A moquito net over the bed and an overhead fan to agitate the air would complete the tropical look.

● A collection of miniature kalanchoes in warm shades of yellow, pink, orange, and red on a bedside table will really glow when lit by a discreet table lamp with a heavy shade.

● A single amaryllis (*Hippeastrum*) on your dressing table can help cheer up those dull winter mornings.

● Choose white moth orchids (*Phalaenopsis*) to go with your pristine, freshly starched Egyptian cotton sheets.

● Place feathery plants near the window to filter the early morning sun, ensuring the gentlest awakening.

Right This dendrobium is just one of many orchids that are suitable for growing in bedrooms. The elegant, arching, canelike stems nod serenely, complementing the quiet elegance.

PRACTICAL PLANTS FOR
BATHROOMS

Modern bathrooms are sanctuaries from stress; more a personal spa than a basic, functional space for a bath. Here, style is as important as in the rest of the house.

Bathroom fittings are now streamlined to encourage pampering and recuperation. The therapeutic soak can be undertaken in a sensual whirlpool bath, or under a power shower generating masses of steam vapor. This steamy environment is the best location for plants that like moisture and humidity.

STYLING IDEAS

Choose one spectacular plant for impact. Something that says in one glance: I am beautiful. This will also reduce clutter: an important consideration in view of the small size of many bathrooms. The rose grape (*Medinilla magnifica*) is perfect. Lush, boldy veined leaves part to display nodding flowers through spring and summer. It is fond of warmth and high humidity but dislikes a draft. This dramatic plant cries out for a similarly exotic container, so look around for a large glazed pot that blends with any other glossy ceramic surface in the bathroom – vivid blue, Chinese red, or shimmering turquoise.

● For a touch of brilliant red look at the flamingo flower (*Anthurium scherzerianium*) and the oilcloth flower (*Anthurium andreanum*). Both are difficult to grow (they need staking), but worth it. The exotic, waxy flowers, with their cheeky curling orange tails, last about two months in spring and summer. They will love the mist.

● Best of all is the gleaming bird's-nest fern (*Asplenium nidus*), which sprouts clumps of bold, long green fronds from a fibrous, nestlike base. It is a magnificently showy plant and deserves to be seen in a good-sized, glossy ceramic container.

● A low-growing, attractive mossy plant that enjoys damp conditions is club moss (*Selaginella*). A shallow pot, filled with well-drained soil, is the ideal way to grow these little beauties. Black and glossy or brash and metallic will make a stylish contrast to the supergreen mass of mossy texture. They dislike direct sun and dry heat, so keep off window ledges and away from radiators.

PLANTING IDEAS

It is important to choose containers that will withstand the damp, steamy atmosphere of a bathroom. Glazed ceramic and most plastic pots are ideal. Those made of cane, bamboo, or wicker will soon show signs of distress unless given a coat of a plant-friendly varnish to protect them from excess moisture.

● African violets (*Saintpaulia*) simply revel in damp conditions. To give them the high humidity they need, try planting them at the base of a large clear glass jar.

● Nearly all the ferns are forest dwellers that actually prefer a damp, steamy environment.

● Try fixing containers of rainforest plants, such as the Christmas cactus (*Schlumbergera*), to the walls of the bathroom to mimic they way the grow in the wild – on trees, well above ground level.

Left The sultry-looking rose grape is an exotic choice for a bathroom. Siting it above the bath, as here, allows you to admire the heavily veined undersides of its leaves and its hanging flowers. It is a perfect focal point for contemplation while you have a relaxing soak.

Steam-loving plants
Bird's nest fern *Asplenium nidus*
Hard fern *Blechnum*
Umbrella grass *Cyperus involucratus*
Boston fern *Nephrolepis exaltata* 'Bostoniensis'
African violet *Saintpaulia*
Christmas cactus *Schlumbergera*

HEALTHY
HOME OFFICES

An increasing number of people are opting to work at home, which opens up a new way of looking at the benefits of houseplants in the home/work arena.

Houseplants are beneficial to the atmosphere: they absorb carbon dioxide from the air and replace it with oxygen via photosynthesis; they act as natural ionizers, helping to eradicate harmful toxins and pollutants from the air (including formaldehyde, found in indoor air) and emissions from computers. *Clivia miniata* – a colorful South African perennial, its flower set apart amidst long and broad dark green leaves – is ideal for a solo feature plant on top of a filing cabinet and is decorative even when out of flower.

PLANT PLACEMENT

Working in a restricted area leaves little space for plants. Here's where the century plant (*Agave americana*) and echeverias are useful. Even small plants can act as space dividers, as shown right. Bushy plants are also useful as room dividers, providing an important psychological barrier between work and play zones, especially if your home office occupies a corner of the living area. When relaxing in the evening, they will help you forget it is there.

Tall, leafy species will hide the desktop computer and files. The weeping fig (*Ficus benjamina*) – one of the most tolerant of all indoor plants – is the best low-maintenance option for this situation. It can reach a good height indoors, and will take up a lot of space when mature. The variegated form 'Variegata' has cream-edged

leaves, so you could place it between two of the regular variety for greater effect. Choose a large container, and water when the soil feels dry. Feed every two weeks and watch it grow. Try not to overwater it, since the leaves will then fall off. Don't despair – new ones will replace them. Keep an eye on the leaves for scale insects. If you find them, wash the bugs off the underside of individual leaves with soapy water – tiresome hand-work, but it is effective.

Think carefully where you put smaller containers, since any water spillage could damage computer or other essential equipment, besides posing the risk of electric shock.

NATURAL IONIZERS

All plants will improve the work environment, but particularly good ionizing plants include:
• Boston fern (*Nephrolepsis exaltata* 'Bostoniensis'), producing a permanent show of soft green fronds.
• Peace lily (*Spathiphyllum wallisii* or *S.* 'Mauna Loa'), with the advantage of white, sail-like flowers of breathtaking purity in spring and summer.
• Tulips (*Tulipa*), hardy bulbs that should be grown in containers outdoors and brought inside for enjoyment just as the flowers are starting to open. Short, sturdy varieties are the best for indoor display. After flowering, they can be planted in the garden.

Right Besides their classic good looks, this agave and trio of echeverias are actually good for your health, absorbing and neutralizing harmful pollutants present in the atmosphere.

Ionizing plants
Maidenhair fern *Adiantum raddianum*
Urn plant *Aechmea fasciata*
Jade plant *Crassula ovata*
Ctenanthe 'Golden Mosaic'
Dumb cane *Dieffenbachia seguine*
Peace lily *Spathiphyllum wallisii*

IDEAS FOR
DISPLAYING PLANTS

Having invested in a stunning plant, you will want to make the most of it; deciding where to place it and how best to display it requires careful consideration.

Left One strong plant and pot can stand alone if they are a special match – here, the dramatic and splashy leaves of the begonia (a rex-cultorum type) cleverly echo the bold pattern of this 1960s ceramic planter.

More often than not, plants are displayed on their own on a coffee table, a kitchen bench, or a windowsill. Larger plants are invariably put on the floor in a corner of the room, where they can all too easily fail to make the statement they should.

With a bit of imagination, plants can be star performers, displaying their beauty in a myriad of positions and under a variety of light conditions. Plants are not just for daytime (see pages 110–17). You must treat the plants you chose as if they are pieces of precious antique china or works of art on display in a gallery.

First, you must set the stage. Look around the room and see which surfaces would suit a tableau of your favorite plants. Piles of illustrated books and decorative ceramic fruit bowls, for example, would complement a wide-lipped container planted with a luxurious pink orchid. Create this look on top of a lacquered console table used to divide a seating area from the rest of the room. You can move this around at any time to alter the ambience of the room.

In hip homes with modern furnishings, go for cool expanses of flooring or shelving, broken up with shots of color provided by foliage or flowering plants. For a dynamic look, display the plants at different levels on modern steel and glass, iron, or wood shelving units –

moving from left to right, beginning with the top, middle, and then the lower section.

Alternatively, look for a display unit that is in keeping with the style of your room, with individual spaces in which to display exotic plants. Each will be quite at home in its own niche. Place the unit against an expanse of plain wall to make the greatest impact, or use it as a room divider, so you can view the plants from both sides.

Unusual furniture such as a French-style delicate wrought-iron table found in an antique market or a slab of marble on top of a wood table make original display surfaces; or place a handmade ceramic tile, a memento from a trip abroad, under the plant.

You can also place plants one under the other on a plant stand, as people did in the 19th century; only update the look by choosing a more modern plant stand (or make one, if you are so inclined) and up-to-the-minute plants. Position flowering plants on top, bushy or trailing plants in the middle, and a compact but colorful plant in the lowest compartment. Place in a corner of a room with reasonable light. Alternatively, you can allow your most treasured plant to take pride of place on the coffee table in the middle of the room, but take care to avoid splashes on the surface when watering.

Top far left The individual boxes on this shelving unit frame a collection of cacti. Although each cactus is an individual, there is a harmony to the arrangement as a trio of different pots and plants are repeated.

Top left Ferns soften the geometric lines of this coffee table.

Bottom far left Corkscrew rushes, in pots that echo the plant's curls in their ridges, are lined up along a table center.

Bottom left One spectacular aloe takes pride of place on this console table.

Right The power of three: identical plants make more of an impact than a selection would.

Left Pretty pansies in a charming trough bring summer indoors.

Top right Shells are used to cover the soil in the pots and also as decorative trim along the edges of the baskets.

Bottom right An antique wrought-iron gate has been made into a plant stand that holds several pots. Look for purpose-designed stands of your chosen period in markets and antique shops.

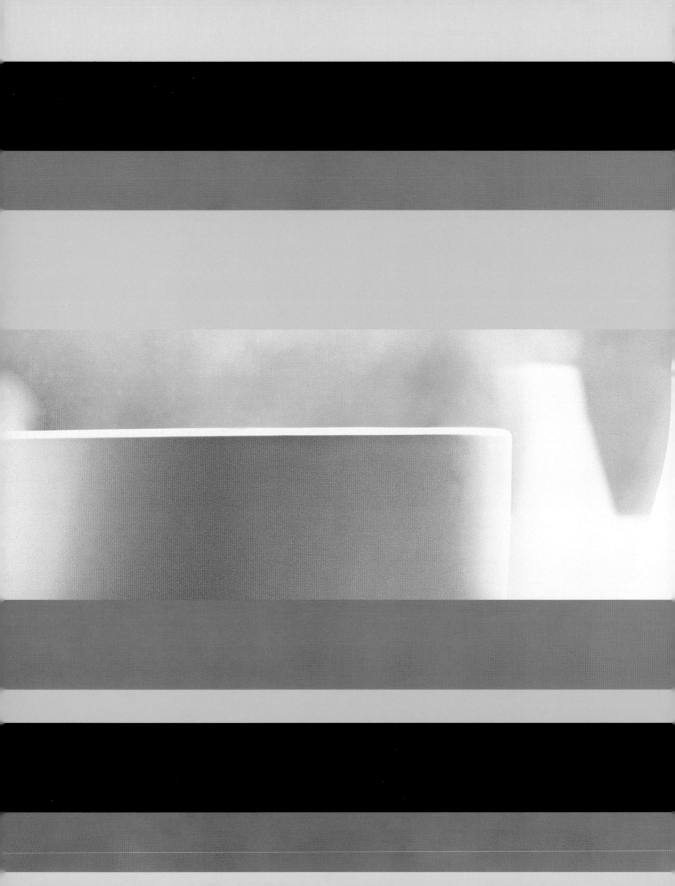

CHOOSING
CONTAINERS

A container is to a plant what a shoe is to a human – it must be able to slip into it comfortably, have extra room for growth, and be of the right style, naturally.

There is such a wealth of variety in containers nowadays that it is easy to link them with the style of the interior. Choose carefully – the shape and size should be in direct proportion to the fully grown plant.

MATERIALS

● Cutting-edge concrete pots may need a hole drilled in the bottom to allow for good drainage. Being unglazed, they are not waterproof. They look good for a while but need looking after.

● Terracotta pots, now available in a wide range of styles and sizes (from tiny to enormous), are porous, and plants potted in them will need regular watering. Soak terracotta pots in water overnight before using.

● Plastic pots retain water and plants will not need watering so frequently. They are often molded to imitate natural materials such as terracotta, stone, or lead, and are generally considerably cheaper than the genuine article.

● Iron-based pots can rust, so check that they have a protective finish when you buy them. When using old iron and metal containers, put the plant in a plain plastic pot and slip that inside.

● Bamboo containers are chic but not that practical, since they tend to split after a while. Slip a plastic pot inside, if necessary, to protect the material against water damage.

● Consider a wooden outer container if you live in a modern space with wood floors.

● Glass containers look sleek and sophisticated and allow you to monitor plant roots. Careful potting can produce a two-tone effect of soil and drainage material.

DRAINAGE

This is the step that will ultimately determine whether you will kill a plant quickly or set it on the road to a healthy life. To enable a plant to drain effectively, line the bottom of your container with small pieces of clay from a broken garden pot, or stones, pebbles, or even styrofoam pieces; this provides a base for the potting soil and the plant's roots. Make sure that this layer is about 2in (5cm) deep. Put the potting mixture on top and then add the plant, pushing the potting mix down as you go. The drainage layer lets the water seep through more quickly than if there were just soil mix on the bottom of the container, which tends to retain moisture. Adding sand to the compost also improves drainage.

● If using a see-through container, be artistic with the drainage layer; turn the container around every now and then to check that the material is even. Empty the container out and repot, if necessary.

● If a pot does not have a hole in the bottom, use a deeper layer of drainage material and add charcoal to the soil mix to keep it sweet.

● If the container is not waterproof line with plastic sheeting; if the pot has drainage holes stand in a saucer.

Right Pure white hand-made pots in unglazed earthenware. Visit small potteries or craft fairs for unique designs.

POTS

CONTAINERS

Top far left Chunkily rustic, these handmade pots are nevertheless supremely practical.

Top left These glazed white pots have a sleek, retro 1950s feel and suit any minimalist interior.

Bottom far left The slippery, glazed insides of these colored pots are actually very beneficial to any plants that need swift drainage.

Bottom left Factory-made terracotta pots are always a reliable choice. Look for slightly taller shapes for a modern feel.

Right Giving pots an initial wash with a water-based paint is a quick way of giving them that customized look.

Left The texture of this silvery-leaved Mexican hat plant perfectly echoes that of the dark concrete container that it is about to be potted into.

Top right Dyed concrete pots are the perfect complement to these campanulas. A top-dressing of white stone chips completes the industrial look.

Bottom right Here, the glossy, hand-shaped leaves of a tree ivy contrast strongly with the containers.

Far left A craftsman-made stone pot such as this one is really unique. Look out for them at craft fairs and galleries or commission one to your own specifications.

Top left Consider the pot's texture: shiny; mat; or strongly patterned. Demand plants that will stand up to their dramatic looks.

Bottom left Handmade pots can be relied on to add a note of distinction to any setting.

Bottom far left Look out for industrial containers – old or new. These galvanized steel boxes make an original choice for a planter.

Bottom left Aluminum and tin containers do not rust but often acquire an attractive patina with age. They make an excellent foil to many houseplants.

Bottom right These terracotta pots have been sprayed silver. Top-dressing the soil with stone chips gives a contemporary finish.

Bottom far right Galvanized and enameled buckets can make superb containers. Put a layer of stone chips in the bottom to aid drainage.

Top far left Lime-washed cylindrical wood pots look like sections of tree-trunk, and are ideal for any collection including African plants.

Top left The textured surface of these balsa wood pots complements the plants' dense mop of leaves.

Bottom far left These smooth, shiny pots are actually made of coconut wood that has been varnished to produce a glassy finish.

Bottom left Teak and mahogany are heavy and substantial materials for plant pots, if expensive. They are strong decorative objects in their own right.

Right Bowls made of bamboo are inexpensive, lightweight, and fresh-looking – making them an ideal way to bring a contemporary note to houseplant collections.

Left These tall, narrow, mat-glazed pots in contrasting cream and black are a sophisticated and modern choice for a wide range of plants.

Top right Rubber and its synthetic equivalents have not been widely used for houseplants, but the modern trend is increasingly to explore the possibilities of such unusual materials.

Bottom right Here, a mat black pot stands on a pair of plinths to show off the elegant, arching lines of the fern.

IMPROVISING
CONTAINERS

Enhance the display of your houseplants by creating original containers from household objects. Transform basic pots with paint, pebbles, moss, or shells.

Containers are important when linking plants to the style of the surroundings, and you can always change them to suit your mood. I like to compare the container or cachepot (an ornamental container for a flowerpot) that houses a plant to the perfect pair of shoes or the essential fashion accessory that round off an outfit.

Often, a simple effect will add drama to an otherwise mundane container – and you don't have to break the bank to achieve impressive results. For example, you could salvage an old colander and use it to plant a practical herb display in the kitchen (see pages 72–73).

Customizing containers can be great fun and need not be intimidating. I am not a great fan of the plain, standard factory-produced terracotta pots which, although inexpensive, lack the character of the hand-thrown versions. However, they are the perfect candidates for customizing, since they are designed for holding plants and are readily available in varying sizes from most shops and garden centers.

Terracotta pots can be painted or sprayed in strong, bold colors for modern environments (see pages 14–15), pastel shades for a more calm and muted setting such as a bedroom, or metallic colors like gold or silver to add a festive note. The results can be enhanced by applying a PVA (polyvinyl acetate) coating which dries to a clear finish and gives the pot a professional look as well as a waterproof covering.

STYLING IDEAS

Provided you consider the drainage aspect and ensure that it is waterproof, don't rule out anything that has the depth or shape to accommodate a plant.

- Transparent vases offer interesting opportunities for transformation. I use a variety of materials, including white stones, pebbles, or shells between the plastic pot and the vase to hide the pot (see right).
- Basic plastic pots can be surrounded by twigs, covered with leaves, or camouflaged with moss.
- I have discovered that leather or woven rattan boxes – often used for the domestic storage of clothing – make wonderful and unusual containers for plants. To make a box waterproof, line it with a piece of heavy-duty plastic covered with a thin layer of gravel to keep it in place.

The improvised containers featured on the opposite page have been conceived around a beachcombing theme. Have fun thinking of themes to suit your home – for example, an industrial look can be achieved by using rows of matching empty food cans stripped of their labels (see pages 72–73).

Top right The addition of twigs and shells "softens" these galvanized containers and gives them a more natural look.

Top far right A glass vase is brought to life by the addition of miniature shells that also camouflage the plastic pot inside.

Bottom right This container was originally a fishing basket. The wire mesh and stones enhance the appeal of this succulent echeveria.

Bottom far right The beading on the edge of the plain basket chimes with the shell trim used to cover the potting soil.

PAINTING POTS

For a unique container, try your hand at painting an ordinary clay pot. Any craft store stocks a wide range of paints and brushes suitable for this endeavor. Most people want to decorate pots in order to produce an individual container in a color or colors that are in harmony with their interior design.

● Decide which style and colors are best by analyzing design features in the room. Which color is dominant? Is there a definite shape and form visible in the furnishings – for instance, does the furniture feature curves or straight lines? You may like to echo the dominant lines in a design on the container.

● Figure painting requires a steady hand. You may prefer to copy a shape onto tracing paper, then transfer the shape to the pot in pencil and, finally, color it in. Keep the shape simple and you will be successful.

● Stripes are easy to paint. Work out the color scheme first on a piece of paper. Place the bare pot on a sheet of newspaper on a worktop and sit down in front of it. If you don't feel very confident, draw pencil lines of where each color is to go around the pot first. Hold the loaded paint brush against the surface of the pot with one hand, and, with the other, rotate the pot at the speed you feel most comfortable with.

Bottom far left Apply a base color of blue and, when dry, stick on tissue paper shapes with PVA. Allow these to dry, then glue on the patches of gold leaf. Once the glue has dried, varnish with a coating of PVA.

Bottom left For this Matisse-inspired pot, first apply two or three base coats of white emulsion. Draw the figures onto blue paper, cut them out, and stick them on with PVA. Apply a couple of coats of PVA to finish the pot.

Bottom right These random stripes on an unglazed terracotta pot are created with acrylic paints. To prevent the colors from running, allow each stripe to dry before adding the next.

Bottom far right Marc Chagall, eat your heart out! First paint on an undercoat of white emulsion. Outline the shapes with black oil pastel, then fill in using oil paints and oil pastels (do not mix the two). Finish with an oil-based varnish.

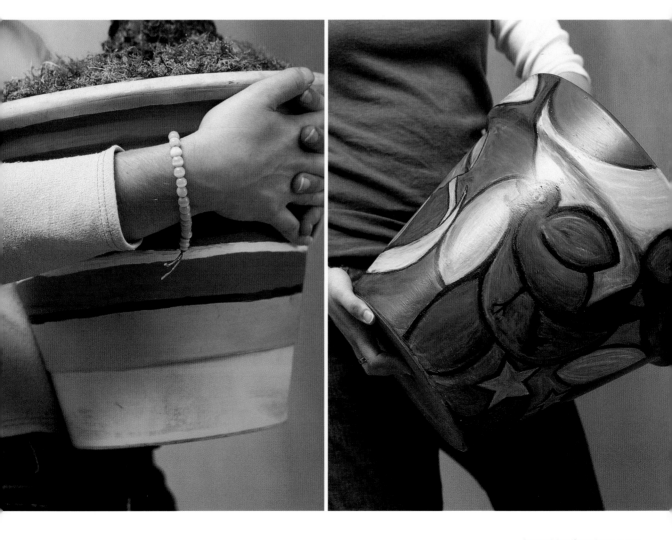

USING
SURFACE TRIMS

The big cover-up of unsightly soil has become a fashion trend and is one to be considered seriously for the added decorative impact it gives.

Regardless of the size and shape of the container, mounds of soil always creep over the rim and lie there, on the tabletop. Adding surface trims is one way of keeping pot plants neat and it adds an extra decorative element, giving you more opportunities to create a stylish planting. However, its real importance is in the practical benefits it brings by preserving moisture in the potting mixture, and helping to keep it warm. It also helps keep the collars of plants dry.

MATERIALS

In recent years, a fantastic array of surface trims has become available through florists' suppliers and specialty stores. As with the containers, the choice of a trim is dictated by the style and growth habit of the plant, as well as the look you are aiming to create.

● Shards of smooth slate provide an option for plants with sturdy stems and foliage that begins a little way up the stems. Look for thin, level slivers that will sit evenly on top of the soil.

● Round black or dark brown pebbles are great with larger, brightly colored plants, providing an attractive contrast. Look for smooth pebbles that fit snugly in the palm of your hand. Coated with a plant-friendly gloss varnish, they will appear permanently wet.

● Traditional moss is still a favorite of many indoor gardeners. It sits happily on top of the soil, bouncing up

and out of the rim – but in a refined way. Be careful not to let it get too dry. Misting occasionally will help keep it fresh and alive.

● Shells from the beach will add a seaside air to a pot, particularly one that's a watery pale or dark blue.

● Opalescent pebbles are best for fragile plants, echoing perhaps their creamy blooms or pale variegated foliage.

● Bark is fabulous under dark foliage plants. It can be a mix of sizes and shapes, but check that it doesn't harbor any pests and is free from signs of mold before adding it to the container.

● Small chips of white, crystal-like stones look cool with cacti, especially in a room with a monochromatic scheme. They suit high-tech metal or highly glazed pots rather well.

● Glass disks take on a new dimension when used as a surface trim for many plants. In a glass or acrylic container they can add color as well as helping to sustain the illusion of transparency.

When adding trim, do not overfill the container or press the trim down too hard on top of the soil. You must allow the soil to breathe and not put pressure on the roots.

Remember that as fashion colors change in both plants and containers, so you can mix and match the trim. Don't throw away old ones, since you never know when the trend will come back.

Top right Fine gravel, small stones, and smashed shells.

Top far right Sphagnum moss is available bagged up at florists and garden centers. Immerse it in water for a while before use, and spray it occasionally to keep it green and fresh.

Bottom right Glass pebbles, both polished and unpolished, are available in a range of jewellike colors.

Bottom far right Polished stones are wonderful just to hold and look at, aside from their practical value as trims.

LIGHTING

NATURAL DAYLIGHT

Plants definitely thrive in natural daylight, growing automatically toward it from wherever they are located in a room.

Plants require light to carry out photosynthesis, which in turn allows them to live a long and healthy life. Certain exotic plants thrive in full sunlight more than others, although not necessarily in direct sunlight, since this can singe the foliage and their delicate blooms. Light enhances flowers; it filters through their colorful petals, creating pale light patterns on surfaces around them. You can almost feel them unfold and revel in the warmth, so if you have a window with a sill deep enough for an extravagant plant that's a perfect focal point, do not hesitate to put it there. If direct sun shines on the window even for ten minutes a day, you should shade the plant with a blind that lets in light but filters the rays.

Take note of where and when the daylight is brightest in the room and place the plants that love those conditions there. A room is darker the closer to the ceiling, so when hanging baskets or placing plants on top of display cabinets and bookshelves, check their growing preferences. Many ivy varieties (*Hedera*) and that wonderful classic plant the leafy aspidistra (*Aspidistra elatior*) are usually happy in this environment.

Moderate light is ideal for most houseplants, which means a spot near a window, but not in strong sunny conditions. If a plant has not been performing well, move it closer to the window and you will soon see it perk up.

In the kitchen, a sunny windowsill is ideal for growing herbs such as basil, sage, and lemon-scented thyme. Keep an eye on the watering regime. Other sunny windowsill plants include cacti, bougainvillea (you can train them to grow in a compact way) and rose geraniums (*Pelargonium* 'Graveolens').

BULBS – GROWING TIPS

Bulbs are storage organs that allow the plant to survive adverse weather conditions by becoming dormant below ground. Amaryllises (*Hippeastrum* hybrids), zantedeschias, and freesias can be grown indoors. Tulips, hyacinths, narcissi, crocuses, and daffodils are actually garden bulbs but can also be grown indoors. Growing bulbs indoors "forces" them to flower well ahead of those in the garden.

● To ensure flowering, buy bulbs from a supplier with a reliable reputation.

● Plant bulbs in August through to October for flowers in January to April.

● For Christmas-flowering hyacinths, plant bulbs in September (northern hemisphere).

● Keep bowls and containers in the dark in a cold place during the root development period, then provide heat and light to promote growth of leaves and flowers.

● Choose tulips with strong stems, and provide some form of support as they grow.

Right Amaryllises and hyacinths are ideal bulbs for a sunny windowsill. Make sure that you rotate the plants regularly so that the stems grow upright – they tend to lean toward the sun. Tall varieties can be top-heavy, and often benefit from staking with a cane or length of thin bamboo.

Other plants for full daylight
Agave victoriae-reginae
Aloe
Paper flower *Bougainvillea*
Desert cacti
Citrus
Echeveria
Euphorbia abyssinica
Olive *Olea europea*

DRAMATIC HALOGEN

Since the advent of the halogen bulb, lighting has brought a new dimension to the concept of spotlighting specific houseplants.

Top left This reading lamp, focussed on a spiky dracaena, lights up the dramatic variegation of its leaves.

Top far left Halogen lamps specifically designed for houseplants can be plunged in the soil surface to create moody shadows on the walls and ceiling.

Bottom left Don't save Christmas tree lights just for the tree! Here, they create a soft, glamorous, Hollywood chic.

Bottom far left The feathery shadows cast by this kentia palm seem to double the plant's size.

Plants for artificial light
Bird's nest fern *Asplenium nidus*
Cast-iron plant *Aspidistra*
   elatior
Dendrobium **hybrids**
Tree ivy *Fatshedera lizei*
Moth orchid *Phalaenopsis*
   hybrids

Lighting in a domestic situation plays an important role in creating atmosphere, be it during the day or at night. It is a subsititute for, as well as an addition to, natural daylight. Halogen fixtures emit a clear white light that is almost like daylight. Clever use creates subtle interplays of light and shade to soften and enhance the decoration of a room. Directional light – the kind provided by a spotlight – picks out the detail, and in the case of houseplants it can really make the foliage come to life and the beauty in the flowers shine through. When directional light is played upon a kentia palm the shadow effects are cast against the wall, revealing the wonderful form of its foliage. It is also useful for highlighting the unique characteristics of a plant such as an amaryllis or exotic bromeliad. Always check if the plant can stand lighting effects. Some foliage is too fragile for the heat that a light bulb of any kind generates, and halogens generate quite a lot.

TYPES OF ARTIFICIAL LIGHT

There are three popular categories:
- Tungsten, the most common form of domestic lighting: a warm light that makes oranges and red seem brighter and blues seem dull.
- Tungsten halogen: a white light that makes blues less dull, and adds a sparkling vitality to a room. Fixtures operate on house voltage and low voltage (usually with a small transformer), and both can be dimmed. Most commonly seen in desklamps and spotlights is the smaller-size halogen reflector bulb.
- Fluorescent: once considerd a harsh light, recent developments have made this more user-friendly.

DESIGNING WITH LIGHT

Depending on the fixture, light can be distributed evenly in all directions, in one direction, or in a concentrated ray. Lighting designers use lights in four different ways: as background lighting, uplighting, task lighting, and accent lighting.
- Background lighting provides a general replacement for daylight and usually comes from a ceiling light (pendant or mounted). The alternatives are wall brackets, free-standing uplights, and table lamps.
- Task lighting is used at kitchen benches and desks in home offices to illuminate work surfaces.
- Accent lighting is mainly used to highlight displays and create a sense of theater. This type is suitable for most houseplants.

Spotlights are usually affixed to the ceiling, beaming a pool of light down, but you can attach them to the wall. Some designs clip to a shelf so they can be moved around. These are also good for lighting plants. Or a track with several lights can be affixed to a ceiling and the spots can move along to highlight individual plants.

CREATIVE
ILLUMINATION

Plants can put on a show-stopping display, and it makes perfect sense to illuminate them in an imaginative and intelligent way.

Informal lighting provided by candles is an acceptable alternative method to electric lighting that allows you to create different moods every time. It's a more fun, relaxed way of illuminating an exciting group of plants. Used imaginatively, the results can be impressive.

Candles are big business and come in a wide range of sizes and colors. Use the same decorating rules that you apply to choosing a plant: does the candle color match or harmonize with the basic color theme? Is the size right – not too overwhelming or too tiny to make an impact? For a romantic mood, choose cream or red (if using potted roses, for instance), and, for party times, use ritzier purples, blues, golds, and silvers.

IDEAS FOR CANDLES

● Make a circle of flames around two or three small pot plants. Choose candles which are lower than the height of the pots.

● Place small, square candles at each corner of a rectangular container, with the height of the candles level with the height of the container.

● Two tall candleholders set in the midst of a group of shorter containers filled with colorful flowers and foliage will enhance the beauty of the grouping.

● Tea lights placed in the bottom of small pots will cast a

soft light over plants. Use them imaginatively (see opposite) – one candle, then one plant placed in a neat row. The plant must have compact growth, as does baby's tears (*Soleirolia soleirolii*).

● For a special event, hang light containers on fine wire next to colorful Chinese lanterns in a location where no one will walk into them (see right).

● Try balancing tiny pots on a large, solid candelabrum. Affix the pots with adhesive, one at each far side, then place a candle in the next branch, on each side, and so on until you reach the top, where you can place the star plant.

CANDLE SAFETY

Of course, you have to take into account the safety issues involved in using fire. A naked flame can easily singe plant leaves, so be careful not to place the candle too close to the plant. Also, do not use a candle in a situation where paper, fabric, or any other flammable material could easily catch fire, and make sure there is someone in the room at all times when the candle is lit.

CANDLE ALTERNATIVES

For a festive occasion, take liberties with tiny Christmas tree lights. You can hang, wrap, and drape them in and around the leaves of tough plants, if it is for a short time only, or around the container.

Top right Schlumbergeras in bud actually look like candles, an impression enhanced by the shallow tray of short candles at their feet.

Top far right A Chinese paper lantern casts a subtle glow.

Bottom right Christmas tree lights have ensnared this dramatic guzmania in flower.

Bottom far right A chorus-line of baby's tears alternating with candles in matching ceramic pots.

PLANT CARE

UNDERSTANDING
SOIL HEALTH

The soil, or potting mixture, is one of the greatest influences on the health and well-being of your plants. It is important to choose the right type and to keep it in good order.

Always buy a good-quality soil mix; cheap ones of dubious origins may contain weed seed or even pests and diseases. They are often old stock in which the fertilizer has broken down and is no longer effective. Garden soil is unsuitable for houseplants. It can also harbor weed seed as well as insect pests and diseases. Within the confines of a pot, soil bacteria can build up to levels that are toxic to plants. Commercial mixes have exactly the right balance of plant nutrients, as well as a loose, light texture.

TYPES OF MIXES

There are several types of mixes. In the first place there is the option of either soil-less or soil-based types. There are advocates for both. In the end, the choice comes down to which you find easiest to use. Some people find they get better results with one rather than the other, while others find it easier to work, particularly with regard to watering, with one particular brand.

- Soil-based mixes are heavy to carry home, but the weight helps to prevent the pots being accidentally knocked over. They are easier to re-water than soil-less ones, should you allow them to dry out.
- Soil-less mixes are lighter to carry but the pots, especially with tall plants in them, can easily fall over if the mix dries out. These mixes can be very difficult to water once they have dried out. (Try adding a bit of dishwashing liquid to the water, should this occur.)

- Fertilizer: soil-less mixes rely entirely on the added fertilizers for their nutrients, whereas the soil-based ones contain a certain amount of nutrient in the soil as well as having some added fertilizers.
- Many soil-less varieties are still based on peat – the use of which many gardeners feel is environmentally unacceptable. If this is an issue for you, look for mixes based on coir or some other renewable resource.

The second choice to be made is regarding the relevance of the mixes. Many plants will cope well with any good potting mix, but others, such as ericaceous plants (azaleas, gardenias, and heathers, for example) or orchids, need a specially formulated mix if they are to thrive. Bromeliads and cacti also need special formulas. It is sometimes advisable (if not always strictly necessary) to add sand, perlite, or vermiculite to standard mix to improve drainage. Plants from woodland areas, such as ferns, often appreciate additions of bark chips to the mix, to simulate the conditions of the forest floor.

Never buy too much mix at any one time. It is not only bulky to store but also it tends to deteriorate on contact with the air, the fertilizer losing its effectiveness. Plan to repot all your plants at the same time and buy just enough mix for the task. After repotting, keep the plants well watered to help them re-establish.

Right Most good-quality proprietary potting mixes have a loose, fibrous, crumbly texture and are sweet-smelling.

CAREFUL
WATERING

Water is essential to any plant's life – without it, it will die, since it will be unable to manufacture food and carry out other essential activities.

Left All living things need water to survive, and learning how much and how often to water your plants is an essential aspect of keeping them healthy. Check your plants daily: you will soon arrive at a regime that suits both you and the plants in your collection.

Drought-tolerant plants

Agave
Aloe
Cast-iron plant *Aspidistra elatior*
Desert cacti
Euphorbia abyssinica
Haworthia

Watering is one of the most important aspects of caring for your indoor plants. A bad watering regime is the cause of far more deaths among indoor plants than either pests or diseases. Most people use tap water for their plants. Generally this is not a problem, although it is always a good idea to fill a watering can and let it stand for several hours before using it. This will allow any chlorine gas to be given off, in addition to ensuring that the water temperature is brought up to that of the room and plant.

The best routine is to refill the can after you have finished watering the plants so that it is ready for your next session. There are a limited number of ericaceous plants, gardenias for example, which do not like alkaline water, which is water containing lime or chalk. In hard water areas there may be sufficient lime in the water to kill the plants. In this situation, it is advisable to collect rain water (in a plastic water barrel) or to use cooled boiled water.

The art of watering is to give the plant just enough. Not enough water and the plant wilts, too much water and the leaves turn yellow and fall off and the plant soon rots. If in doubt, err on the side of less rather than more water. To water from below, stand the plant in a dish of water and allow the soil to suck up the water. This has the advantage of not wetting the leaves or crown of the plant. For soil-less mixes that have completely dried out this may be the only

method of re-wetting the soil. The other method is to water from above with a watering can. Soak the soil mix thoroughly and allow excess to drain away. Do not water again until the mix is almost dry and then wet thoroughly again. Do not water if the mix is already wet. During the dormant season, when a plant is resting, use only a little water, so that the soil is barely moist.

Some plants (notably orchids, African violets, and other plants that originate in rain forests) appreciate high humidity, and the best way of achieving this is to mist the plants once or twice a day while they are in active growth. Alternatively, stand the pots on trays of wetted clay pellets (available from garden centers) that release moisture around the plant gradually.

There are various aids to make your watering regime easier, including self-watering containers as well as water-retaining granules or crystals that can be added to the mix. Some people find these a great help, others fail to get on with them and prefer to rely on manual watering, over which they feel they have more control.

When on vacation, ask a friend to keep an eye on your plants for you. Grouping all the plants together in a spot sheltered from hot sun will raise the humidity around them, and the soil mix will dry out more slowly.

REGULAR
FEEDING

Plants – like humans – need food to keep them alive. As the owner of a houseplant, it is entirely up to you to keep it on the planet.

Most of your houseplants' requirements are manufactured by the plant using water and sunlight, as well as the carbon dioxide in the atmosphere, a process known as photosynthesis. However, there are a number of nutrients that are also essential to its healthy well-being. In the open garden many of these are contained within the soil or added by the application of organic matter (vegetable remains that break down in the soil). In the indoor garden, they have to be added artificially in the form of fertilizer or plant feed. Although all soil mixes contain some fertilizer in their make-up, much of this is either used up or washed out (leeched) by the continual passage of water through the mix from regular irrigation. It is vital to replace this if you want to keep your plants healthy.

There are several ways of doing this. One is to add solid fertilizer to the soil mix and the second is to provide it in a soluble form added to the water at watering time. Solid fertilizer comes in several different forms. The current favorite is what is known as a slow-release fertilizer. When added to the soil, this takes several months to break down, gently releasing its nutrients over the whole period. This reduces feeding to only once or twice a year. These slow-release fertilizers may come in granules which are mixed into the soil or as a "plug" or a "spike", a cluster of granules that are stuck together, which is inserted whole just below the surface.

An alternative method is to use a liquid feed. This is added to the water in prescribed quantities and applied at regular intervals as stated on the label of the container. A variant to this is a foliar feed, whereby the feed is added to water but it is then sprayed onto the foliage rather than poured with a watering can into the soil. The fertilizer is then absorbed by the plant through its leaves. This is a useful way for prescribing a quick pick-me-up for an ailing plant, since the nutrients are immediately available.

Most plants are happy with a general or standard fertilizer. Such fertilizers are often described as "balanced": the main plant nutrients, nitrogen, phosphorus, and potassium, are present in equal amounts. There are also specific ones for specific plants. A tomato liquid feed, which is high in potassium, is often a good choice for encouraging flowering plants – particularly orchids – to bloom.

The frequency with which you feed will depend on the type of fertilizer you are using, but details are always given on the packaging. You should only feed a plant when it is producing new leaves. Some products need to be diluted, but some are available ready-mixed, and these are obviously preferable if you are short on time. Do not exceed the recommended dose. Excess fertilizer can be toxic to plants. Plants that are dormant or resting, generally during the winter months, do not require any feed.

Right Fertilizers are magic potions, keeping your houseplants healthy and helping them to perform at their optimum. If you need to dilute the fertilizer, always follow the manufacturer's instructions. Do not store excess feed. You should also not introduce any surplus into the public drainage system: dispose of it by watering it over a path or driveway.

Don't need to feed these
Cast-iron plant *Aspidistra elatior*
Hard fern *Blechnum*
Spider plant *Chlorophytum comosum* 'Vittatum'
Guzmania lingulata
Hyacinth *Hyacinthus orientalis* hybrids
Hydrangea *Hydrangea macrophylla* hybrids

TIME FOR
REPOTTING

Indoor plants should not be left indefinitely in the same soil mix – change it for fresh at least once a year to give your plants a new lease of life.

Top far left The roots of this plant have emerged from the base of the pot. Potting on is well overdue.

Top left Slide the plant from the container. If the roots are very congested, as here, it may be necessary to cut off the old pot with scissors.

Bottom far left Prepare the new container by putting a layer of sand, small stones, or pot shards at the base.

Bottom left Holding the plant in the center of the pot, feed in fresh soil around the sides with your other hand.

For a growing plant this means potting on into a larger pot, but for mature plants that have reached their maximum pot size it means replacing some or all of the soil and returning the plant either to the same pot or to one of a similar size.

When a young plant is first introduced to a pot this is known as "potting" or "potting up". A seedling, cutting, or division is put into a pot that will just accommodate its root ball. Never place a plant into too large a pot immediately. Water will collect in the soil not occupied by plant roots, leading to stagnant conditions. Place some drainage material such as pot shards, stones, or gravel in the bottom of the pot to allow free drainage. Put some soil on top of this and then suspend the plant in the center of the pot with one hand while filling it with soil with the other. Firm it down so that the final level of soil is level with the original planting depth of the young plant. Be sure to leave a gap between the soil surface and the rim of the pot – up to 1in (2.5cm) should be sufficient – to allow for watering. Press a fertilizer plug into the soil mix so it sits just below the soil surface and water the pot thoroughly.

As the plant grows, the roots begin to fill the pot. Never allow this to get to the point where the roots are tightly wound around the inside of the pot. (However, some flowering plants, such as clivias, appreciate being a little

pot-bound: the stress seems to make them flower their hearts out.) Just as the roots begin to circle around the sides of the pot (roots will often also show through the drainage holes at this stage), remove the plant from its container and "pot on". Use the next size of container up, having first placed a layer of drainage material in the bottom. Also place a layer of the appropriate soil mix in the bottom so that the top of the original root ball comes just below the rim of the pot. Fill in the gap around the root ball with fresh soil and water to settle the plant in.

Continue to pot on in this way every year until the plant is in the largest pot or until it has finished growing. At this stage it becomes necessary to "repot" into the same size pot. If possible, remove the plant from the pot and then scrape way as much of the soil as you can without disturbing the roots too much. Repot the plant in the normal way into the same pot or into a new one of the same size. If you are returning the plant to the same pot, scrub it out first with a mild, plant-friendly disinfectant to kill off any bacteria.

If the pot or the plant is too large for you to be able to remove the plant easily, tilt it on its side and scrape away as much of the surface soil as you are able to and then replace this with fresh soil. This process is generally referred to as topdressing.

DEALING WITH
PESTS & DISEASES

Many indoor gardeners become worried about the problems of pests and diseases. Don't fret unduly – just follow the advice below.

Given healthy conditions and good soil mix there should be few problems caring for houseplants. Having said that, it is as well to be prepared for any problems that might occur.

PREVENTIVE CARE

If you follow this advice the chances of problems will be reduced considerably:

- Check all new plants before bringing them into your home to make sure that they are not themselves carrying pests or diseases.
- Feed and water plants correctly and make sure that the soil is in good condition.
- Keep plants in a light, airy place that is not in a draft or hot sunlight.
- Remove dead leaves and spent flowers immediately, as these can harbor fungi.
- The best defense against both pests and diseases is to make sure that the plants are healthy. Starved, sickly plants are far more susceptible to passing ailments than those that have been looked after.

PESTS

Always check your plants when you water them to make sure that there are no pests lurking among the leaves. If caught at an early stage, most can be picked off with the fingers or a pair of tweezers. Alternatively, wash them off with a spray of soapy water. If the outbreak has become severe before you notice it, the only really satisfactory way of coping with it is to use a relevant chemical spray. Insecticides are changing all the time, so check with your garden center as to which is best formulated to solve your problem. Do not drench the whole plant but concentrate on the area infested by the insects. Stop as soon as the infestation has been eradicated.

In the open garden, beneficial insects such as ladybugs and lacewings are useful biological controls, since they attack pests such as aphids. These are not so useful for houseplants, although they might work in greenhouses and conservatories where there is a wide variety of flowering plants and plenty of open windows. However, if you want to avoid chemicals, there are other forms of biological control that can be used against specific pests, and these can be ordered with advice from garden centers.

DISEASES

Good hygiene, healthy plants, and vigilance, including the removal of any damaged or bruised leaves and stems and dusting the cuts with a fungicide, will reduce the risk of diseases. Regular examination can preempt major outbreaks of a disease, leaving the use of chemicals as almost the last resort. The final solution is to throw the plant away and replace it with a healthy specimen.

Right Ladybugs are beneficial creatures that feed on insect pests. They do not normally find their way indoors, so it is worth opening a few windows occasionally or placing your plants outdoors in good weather to take advantage of these charming do-gooders.

Bad bugs
Whitefly
Aphids
Spider mites
Scale insects
Mealybugs

Diseases
Downy mildew
Powdery mildew
Sooty mold
Viruses
Rusts
Leaf spots
Verticillium wilt

PLANT **MAINTENANCE**

☼ **Light**
🌡 **Temperature**
💧 **Feeding**
💧 **Watering**
⊟ **Soil mix**

Adiantum raddianum *Maidenhair fern*
Height to 24in (60cm), spread 32in (80cm)
These elegant ferns are ideal for growing either on their own or with other houseplants. They appreciate humidity, so make good bathroom plants ☼ Bright indirect light in summer, bright filtered light in winter 🌡 No lower than 45˚F (7˚C) in winter 💧 Green houseplant fertilizer every 4 weeks in spring and summer 💧 Freely when in growth, sparingly in winter; stand plants on trays of wetted pebbles to increase humidity ⊟ Standard fern soil mix

Aechmea fasciata *Urn plant*
Height to 16in (40cm), spread 20in (50cm)
Urn plants have showy, bright sugar-pink and mauve flowers in summer, but their thick, strap-shaped, silvery gray leaves are attractive throughout the year ☼ Bright filtered light 🌡 No lower than 50˚F (10˚C) in winter 💧 Flowering houseplant fertilizer every 4 weeks in spring and summer 💧 Keep the central "cup" filled with soft water ⊟ Standard bromeliad soil mix

Aechmea nudicaulis
Height to 28in (70cm), spread 10in (25cm)
These plants have shiny, straplike leaves and yellow flowers that are surrounded by showy red bracts in summer ☼ Bright filtered light 🌡 No lower than 50˚F (10˚C) in winter 💧 Flowering houseplant fertilizer every 4 weeks in spring and summer 💧 Keep the central "cup" filled with soft water ⊟ Standard bromeliad soil mix

Agave victoriae-reginae
Height to 20in (50cm), spread 20in (50cm)
These succulents have thick, spiny leaves. Curving spikes of creamy-white flowers, sometimes tinged purple, appear in summer ☼ Full light 🌡 No lower than 50˚F (10˚C) in winter 💧 Flowering houseplant fertilizer every 4 weeks in spring and summer 💧 Water freely in spring and summer, less in autumn, and sparingly in winter ⊟ Standard cactus soil mix

Alocasia sanderiana *Elephant's ear plant*
Height to 6ft (2m), spread 6ft (2m)
These dramatic foliage plants have large wavy leaves margined with silver and with a pronounced metallic sheen ☼ Filtered light 🌡 No lower than 59˚F (15˚C) in winter 💧 Apply a balanced fertilizer every 2–3 weeks when in growth 💧 Freely in spring and summer, moderately in winter ⊟ Soil-based potting mix with added sand and composted bark

Aloe aristata *Lace aloe*
Height to 5in (12cm), spread 5in (12cm)
These succulents have thick, pointed leaves with pronounced white spots ☼ Full light 🌡 No lower than 50˚F (10˚C) in winter 💧 Apply a balanced fertilizer every 8 weeks in spring and summer 💧 Moderately throughout the year, but sparingly when dormant ⊟ Standard soil mix with added sharp sand or perlite

Aloe variegata *Partridge-breasted aloe*
Height to 8in (20cm), spread 8in (20cm)
Succulents with thick, fleshy leaves broadly banded with silver ☼ Full light 🌡 No lower than 50˚F (10˚C) in winter 💧 Apply a balanced fertilizer every 8 weeks in spring and summer 💧 Moderately throughout the year, but sparingly when dormant ⊟ Standard soil mix with added sharp sand or perlite

Aloe vera
Height to 24in (60cm), spread 24in (60cm)
Widely used in the cosmetics industry, this succulent also makes an attractive houseplant. It is tolerant of a certain amount of neglect ☼ Full light 🌡 No lower than 50˚F (10˚C) in winter 💧 Apply a balanced fertilizer every 8 weeks in spring and summer 💧 Moderately throughout the year, but sparingly when dormant ⊟ Standard soil mix with added sharp sand or perlite

Aphelandra squarrosa *Zebra plant*
Height to 12in (30cm), spread 12in (30cm)
This dramatic houseplant is grown for its white-ribbed leaves and spikes of yellow flowers ☼ Full light, filtered in summer 🌡 No lower than 45˚F (7˚C) in winter, but better kept warmer 💧 Feed with a balanced fertilizer every 2 weeks in summer, every 4 weeks in winter 💧 Apply soft water freely when in growth, more sparingly in winter ⊟ Standard soil mix

Aspidistra elatior *Cast-iron plant*
Height to 24in (60cm), spread 24in (60cm)
Among the easiest houseplants to grow, aspidistras are tough plants that seem to withstand any amount of neglect ☼ Bright filtered light, but tolerates shadier positions 🌡 Ideally no lower than 45˚F (7˚C) in winter 💧 Apply a balanced fertilizer every 4 weeks when in growth 💧 Moderately when in growth, sparingly in winter ⊟ Standard soil mix

Asplenium nidus *Bird's nest fern*
Height to 5ft (1.5m), spread 3ft (1m)
These ferns have glossy, straplike leaves that curl at the tips ☼ Bright filtered light 🌡 No lower than 50˚F (10˚C) in winter 💧 Apply a balanced fertilizer at half strength every 4 weeks when in growth 💧 Freely when in growth, sparingly in winter ⊟ Standard soil mix with added peat substitute, sharp sand, and charcoal

Begonia x tuberhybrida *Tuberhybrida begonia*
Height and spread variable depending on the variety grown; some have trailing stems and are good in hanging baskets
Tuberous begonias, which are completely dormant in winter, are grown for their luminous flowers in shades of white, pink, yellow, orange, and red over a long period in summer to early autumn ☼ Bright light with shade from direct sun 🌡 Store in a frost-free place when dormant in winter 💧 Apply a balanced fertilizer every second watering when in growth 💧 Freely when in growth; keep dry in winter ⊟ Standard soil mix

Begonia 'Norah Bedson'
Height to 9in (23cm), spread 10in (25cm)
A so-called rhizomatous begonia, this has red-speckled stems and mottled leaves ☼ Bright light with shade from direct sun 🌡 No lower than 50˚F (10˚C) in winter 💧 Apply a balanced fertilizer every second watering when in growth 💧 Freely when in growth; keep dry in winter ⊟ Standard soil mix

Begonia (rex-cultorum types) *Painted-leaf begonia*
Height to 24in (60cm), spread 24in (60cm), depending on the species
Rex begonias are grown for their brilliantly colored leaves, which often have a metallic sheen. The flowers are inconspicuous

☼ Bright light with shade from direct sun 🌡 No lower than 50°F (10°C) in winter 💧 Apply a balanced fertilizer every second watering when in growth ◊ Freely when in growth; keep dry in winter 🪴 Standard soil mix

Blechnum species *Hard fern*
Height and spread depend on the species but usually to 12in (30cm) when grown as a houseplant
These handsome ferns appreciate high humidity and therefore make a good choice for a kitchen or bathroom. In time, they develop a woody stem at the crown
☼ Bright filtered or indirect light 🌡 No lower than 64°F (18°C) in winter 💧 Not necessary ◊ Water freely when in growth, moderately in winter 🪴 Standard soil mix with added bark, charcoal, and sharp sand

Bougainvillea hybrids *Paper flower*
Height to 15ft (5m), spread 15ft (5m), less in a container
These showy climbers are grown not for their true flowers, which are inconspicuous, but for the white, pink, red, or salmon orange bracts that surround them. They are best given some support. The stems are thorny
☼ Full light 🌡 No lower than 32°F (0°C) in winter 💧 Apply a balanced fertilizer every 4 weeks when in growth ◊ Water freely when in growth, and keep just moist in winter 🪴 Standard soil mix

Bouvardia hybrids
Height to 36in (90cm), spread 24in (60cm)
These shrubby plants usually flower from late summer into winter. Some varieties have scented flowers
☼ Bright filtered light 🌡 No lower than 41°F (5°C) in winter 💧 Apply a balanced fertilizer every 4 weeks when in growth, but not when flowering ◊ Water freely when in growth, keep just moist in winter 🪴 Standard soil mix

Brassica oleracea *Ornamental cabbage*
Height to 18in (45cm), spread to 18in (45cm)
Ornamental cabbages and kales are annual plants that are at their best in autumn and winter. They color best at low temperatures, so keep them outdoors for most of the time, bringing them inside for short spells only
☼ Bright light with shade from direct sun 🌡 Ideally below 50°F (10°C); higher temperatures are tolerated for short periods 💧 Apply a balanced fertilizer every 4 weeks in growth ◊ Freely when in growth 🪴 Standard soil mix

CACTI
Height to 12in (30cm), spread 6in (15cm), but depends on the species and the age of the plant
Desert cacti are grown for the fascination of their overall appearance. Some are tall and slender, others almost globular, and nearly all are spiny. Not all will flower as young plants. Most are slow-growing
☼ Full light 🌡 No lower than 45°F (7°C) in winter, though some will tolerate short spells at near freezing 💧 When in growth, apply cactus fertilizer every 4–5 weeks ◊ In growth, soak thoroughly with soft water and allow to dry out between waterings; keep dry in winter 🪴 Cactus soil mix

Calathea species
Height and spread variable depending on the species, but usually within 3ft (1m).
These foliage plants are adapted to low light levels, so make excellent houseplants. They need high humidity
☼ Bright indirect or filtered light 🌡 No lower than 61°F (16°C) in winter 💧 Apply a balanced liquid fertilizer every 4 weeks when in growth ◊ Freely when in growth, moderately in winter; mist daily 🪴 Standard soil mix

Campanula isophylla *Falling stars*
Height to 8in (20cm), spread 12in (30cm)
With numerous light blue or white flowers in mid-summer, these make excellent subjects for pots and hanging baskets
☼ Bright filtered light 🌡 No lower than 32°F (0°C) in winter 💧 In growth, apply a balanced feed every 4 weeks ◊ In growth, water freely; keep moist in winter 🪴 Standard soil mix

Capsicum annuum *Chili pepper, paprika*
Height to 12in (30cm), spread 12in (30cm)
Except for their uses in the kitchen, these make attractive indoor plants, with their showy white, yellow, orange, red, or purple fruits
☼ Bright filtered light 🌡 No lower than 39°F (4°C) in winter 💧 Feed with a balanced fertilizer every 10 days when in growth until the fruits start to color ◊ Water freely when in growth, sparingly in winter 🪴 Standard soil mix

Chlorophytum comosum 'Vittatum' *Spider plant*
Height to 8in (20cm) or more, spread 12in (30cm) or more
These familiar plants are extremely tolerant and will grow in a variety of situations; they are excellent in hanging baskets

☼ Bright indirect to full light, but shaded from hot sun 🌡 No lower than 45°F (7°C) in winter 💧 Apply a green foliage plant fertilizer every 4 weeks when in growth ◊ Water freely when in growth, moderately in winter 🪴 Standard soil mix

Citrus species *Orange, lemon, lime, etc.*
Height to 6ft (2m), spread 3ft (1m)
These evergreen shrubs have intoxicatingly scented flowers that open at the same time as the previous year's fruits are ripening. Plants can be clipped over to keep them within bounds
☼ Full light, but shaded from hot sun 🌡 No lower than 37°F (3°C) in winter 💧 Apply balanced liquid fertilizer every 2–3 weeks when in growth ◊ In growth water freely and mist daily; water sparingly in winter 🪴 Standard soil mix

Clivia miniata *Kaffir lily*
Height to 18in (45cm), spread 12in (30cm)
Among the easiest flowering houseplants to grow, clivias have showy orange flowers in spring, carried on strong stems above the arching, straplike leaves. They flower best when pot-bound
☼ Bright filtered or indirect light 🌡 No lower than 50°F (10°C) in winter 💧 Apply a balanced fertilizer every 4 weeks when in growth (but not when the flower buds are forming) ◊ Freely when in growth, moderately in winter 🪴 Standard soil mix with added sand or perlite

Codiaeum hybrids *Croton*
Height to 36in (90cm), spread 24in (60cm)
These houseplants are grown for their brilliantly colored, leathery leaves. The flowers are inconspicuous
☼ Full light with shade from hot sun 🌡 No lower than 46°F (8°C) in winter 💧 In growth, apply a balanced fertilizer every 2–3 weeks ◊ In growth, water freely and mist daily; water sparingly in winter with tepid water 🪴 Standard soil mix

Convallaria majalis *Lily-of-the-valley*
Height to 9in (23cm), spread 12in (30cm)
Lily-of-the-valley is a hardy garden plant that can be forced in containers to produce its deliciously scented flowers indoors in late winter. Pot plants up in autumn and keep in moderate heat to accelerate growth; return to the garden after flowering
☼ Bright indirect light 🌡 No lower than 32°F (0°C) in winter 💧 Apply a flowering houseplant fertilizer when in growth until the flower buds form ◊ Freely when in growth 🪴 Standard soil mix

Cyclamen persicum hybrids *Florists' cyclamen*

Height to 8in (20cm), spread 6in (15cm)

These cyclamen have been bred as houseplants that flower in autumn and winter. The flowers, which have distinctive swept-back petals, can be white, pink, glowing red, or purple. They appreciate cool conditions

☼ Bright filtered light, full light in winter ▮ No lower than 55°F (13°C) in winter ♦ Flowering houseplant fertilizer every 2 weeks when in leaf ◊ Freely when in growth (but not directly over the tuber); keep dry when dormant in summer ▦ Standard soil mix

Cyperus involucratus *Umbrella grass*

Height to 24in (60cm), spread 24in (60cm)

This grassy plant grows in water in the wild, but is eminently suitable for growing as a houseplant if given sufficient moisture

☼ Bright filtered light ▮ No lower than 41°F (5°C) in winter ♦ Apply a balanced fertilizer every 4 weeks in summer ◊ Water freely and stand containers in shallow trays of water ▦ Standard soil mix

Dendrobium hybrids

Height to 24in (60cm), spread 12in (30cm)

These orchids are mainly spring-flowering

☼ Lightly shaded from late spring to summer; full light from autumn to early spring ▮ No lower than 50°F (10°C) in winter ♦ Apply an orchid fertilizer at every 3rd watering when in growth ◊ When in growth, water freely and mist twice daily; keep dry in winter ▦ Epiphytic orchid mix

Dieffenbachia seguine 'Exotica' *Dumb cane*

Height to 3ft (1m), spread 16in (40cm)

The large leaves of this plant are generously splashed and mottled with creamy white. It is one of a large number of selected forms of the species

☼ Bright filtered light; full light in winter ▮ No lower than 59°F (15°C) in winter ♦ In growth, apply a balanced fertilizer every 4 weeks ◊ In growth, water moderately and mist daily; water sparingly in winter ▦ Standard soil mix

Dracaena fragrans Deremensis Group

Height to 15ft (5m), spread 3ft (1m), often less in a container

These shrubby plants branch with age and can become tree-like. They are grown for their strikingly variegated leaves

☼ Full light, shaded from direct sun ▮ No lower than 55°F (13°C) in winter ♦ From spring to autumn, apply a balanced fertilizer every 4 weeks ◊ Freely when in growth, sparingly in winter ▦ Standard soil mix

Echeveria species

Height to 6in (15cm), spread 12in (30cm), depending on the species

These succulents form rosettes of fleshy leaves. The tall, arching flower spikes are of secondary interest

☼ Full light ▮ No lower than 45°F (7°C) in winter ♦ In growth, apply a balanced fertilizer at half strength every 4 weeks ◊ In growth, water moderately; keep just moist in winter ▦ Standard cactus mix

Euphorbia abyssinica

Height to 4ft (1.2m), spread 18in (45cm)

This almost tree-like succulent looks like a cactus, with its curious angled stems

☼ Full light ▮ No lower than 54°F (12°C) in winter ♦ In growth, apply a balanced fertilizer at half strength every 2 weeks ◊ In growth, water moderately; keep just moist in winter ▦ Standard soil mix with added sand

Fatshedera lizei *Tree ivy*

Height to 4ft (1.2m), spread to 10ft (3m)

These tolerant shrubs (hybrids of fatsia and ivy) are actually hardy enough to be grown outdoors in most climates, but also make dramatic houseplants

☼ Most situations are acceptable, but shade from hot summer sun ▮ Tree ivies will survive lows of -23°F (5°C) ♦ In growth, apply a balanced fertilizer every 4 weeks ◊ Freely when in growth, sparingly in winter ▦ Standard soil mix

Ficus benjamina *Weeping fig*

Height to 5ft (1.5m), spread 4ft (1.2m)

Easily grown shrubs that, given the right conditions, can exceed the dimensions given here

☼ Full or filtered light ▮ No lower than 59°F (15°C) in winter ♦ In growth, apply a green foliage plant fertilizer every 4 weeks ◊ Freely when in growth, moderately at other times ▦ Standard soil mix with added fine bark chips

Ficus lyrata *Banjo fig, fiddle-leaf fig*

Height to 6ft (2m), spread 18in (45cm)

This foliage plant has fiddle-shaped, glossy green leaves that are roughly corrugated. An excellent foil to flowering plants

☼ Bright or filtered light ▮ No lower than 59°F (15°C) in winter ♦ In growth, apply a foliage houseplant fertilizer every 4 weeks ◊ Freely when in growth, moderately at other times ▦ Standard soil mix with added fine bark chips

Gardenia augusta *Gardenia*

Height to 18in (45cm), spread 18in (45cm)

The glossy, rich green leaves offset the sweetly scented, white flowers in summer and autumn

☼ Bright filtered light ▮ No lower than 50°F (10°C) in winter ♦ In growth, apply a balanced fertilizer every 4 weeks ◊ In growth, water freely with soft water; keep barely moist in winter ▦ Ericaceous soil mix

Gerbera jamesonii hybrids *Transvaal daisy*

Height to 18in (45cm), spread 24in (60cm)

These plants have long-lasting, brilliantly colored daisy flowers (cream, yellow, apricot, orange, and pink) over a long period from spring to autumn but are sometimes forced to flower at other times of year.

☼ Bright filtered light ▮ No lower than 41°F (5°C) in winter ♦ In growth, apply a balanced fertilizer every 4 weeks ◊ Water freely when in growth; keep moist in winter ▦ Standard soil mix

Guzmania lingulata *Scarlet star*

Height to 18in (45cm), spread 18in (45cm)

In winter, this bromeliad has brilliant orange-red or scarlet bracts that surround the true flowers

☼ Bright filtered or indirect light ▮ No lower than 59°F (15°C) in winter ♦ None required ◊ In growth, mist daily with soft water; in winter, keep the soil barely moist and do not mist ▦ Bromeliad soil mix

Hibiscus rosa-sinensis hybrids *Rose of China*

Height to 5ft (1.5m), spread 3ft (1m)

These fast-growing shrubs have bright glossy green leaves and flowers in shades of crimson, orange, yellow, and white

☼ Bright filtered light ▮ No lower than 50°F (10°C) in winter ♦ In growth, apply a balanced fertilizer every 4 weeks ◊ Freely when in growth, sparingly in winter ▦ Standard soil mix

Hippeastrum hybrids *Amaryllis*

Height to 12–20in (30–50cm), spread 12in (30cm)

These bulbs are usually forced to flower in late winter. Flower colors include white, pink, and red; selected forms can have double or bi-colored flowers

☼ Bright filtered or full light ▮ No lower than 55°F (13°C) in winter ♦ Feed with a balanced fertilizer every 2 weeks after flowering until the leaves start to die back ◊ Freely when in growth; keep dry when dormant ▦ Standard soil mix or bulb fiber; plant with the neck of the bulb just above the soil surface

Howea fosteriana *Kentia palm*

Height to 8ft (2.5m), spread 6ft (2m)

These dramatic-looking palms seem to thrive in a variety of positions in the home and are apparently indestructible

☼ Full light ▮ No lower than 59°F (15°C) in winter

In growth, apply a balanced fertilizer monthly
Moderately when in active growth, sparingly at other times ⊞ Standard soil mix

Hyacinthus orientalis hybrids *Hyacinth*
Height to 12in (30cm), spread 3in (8cm)
With deliciously scented flowers in shades of white, pink, blue, purple, red, and salmon orange, hyacinths retain their popularity. Specially prepared bulbs have been forced to flower in winter. After flowering, they can be planted in the garden, but may take a season or two to recover
☼ Keep bulbs for forcing in the dark for 6 weeks until the shoots are 1in (2.5cm) long, then bring them into full light ⫤ No higher than 45°F (7°C) when kept dark; then at room temperature
None necessary ⟳ Water carefully to avoid waterlogging the shoots ⊞ Bulb fiber

Hydrangea macrophylla hybrids *Hydrangea*
Height to 3ft (1m), spread 3ft (1m)
These hardy shrubs normally flower in mid-summer, but are often forced into flower at other times and sold as houseplants. They are unsuitable for growing in the home environment indefinitely: after flowering, cut them back and keep them in containers outdoors or plant them in the open garden
☼ Bright indirect light ⫤ No lower than 32°F (0°C)
Slow-release fertilizer after flowering ⟳ Water freely while in active growth ⊞ Standard soil mix

Isolepis cernua (syn. Scirpus cernuus) *Slender club-rush*
Height to 8in (20cm), spread 18in (45cm)
This grass-like plant is usually trailing and is therefore suitable for a hanging basket, but can be trimmed back with scissors for a neater, more funky appearance
☼ Bright filtered light ⫤ No lower than 50°F (10°C) in winter In growth, apply a green houseplant fertilizer every 4 weeks ⟳ Water freely in growth; keep moist in winter ⊞ Standard soil mix

Jasminum polyanthum *Jasmine*
Height to 3ft (1m), spread 2ft (60cm), but depends on the support used
This climber has deliciously fragrant flowers in late winter to early spring. Though delicate-looking, it is surprisingly vigorous. It needs some support – a hoop of either cane or wire plunged into the soil surface is best
☼ Bright filtered light or full light with shade from hot sun ⫤ No lower than 32°F (0°C) in winter
In growth, apply a flowering houseplant fertilizer every 4 weeks ⟳ In growth, water freely, sparingly in winter ⊞ Standard soil mix

Juncus effusus 'Spiralis' *Corkscrew rush*
Height to 18in (45cm), spread 24in (60cm)
This bizarre plant is grown for the appeal of its spiralling, shiny dark green stems
☼ Full light ⫤ No lower than 32°F (0°C) in winter
Apply a balanced fertilizer every 4 weeks when in growth ⟳ Water freely throughout the year to keep permanently moist ⊞ Standard soil mix

Kalanchoe daigremontiana *Mexican hat plant*
Height to 3ft (1m), spread 12in (30cm)
This succulent has fleshy gray leaves with toothed margins, but its principal attraction is its method of reproduction – tiny new plantlets are produced all along the leaf edges
☼ Bright filtered light ⫤ No lower than 50°F (10°C) in winter Apply a balanced liquid fertilizer every 4 weeks when in active growth ⟳ Freely from spring to autumn, keep just moist in winter ⊞ Standard soil mix with added sand

Kalanchoe hybrids *Flaming Katy*
Height to 12in (30cm), spread 12in (30cm)
Familiar plants with glossy, succulent-looking green leaves and clusters of red, yellow, pink, or orange flowers in winter and spring
☼ Bright filtered light ⫤ No lower than 50°F (10°C) in winter Apply a balanced liquid fertilizer every 4 weeks when in active growth ⟳ Freely from spring to autumn, keep just moist in winter ⊞ Standard soil mix with added sand

Kalanchoe thyrsiflora
Height to 24in (60cm), spread 12in (30cm)
This succulent has red-margined, pale green leaves and clusters of fragrant yellow flowers in spring
☼ Bright filtered light ⫤ No lower than 54°F (12°C) in winter Apply a balanced liquid fertilizer every 4 weeks when in active growth ⟳ Freely from spring to autumn, keep just moist in winter ⊞ Standard soil mix with added sand

Lavandula species *Lavender*
Height to 2ft (60cm), spread 18in (45cm)
A number of different lavenders are grown, all with narrow, characteristically aromatic, gray-green leaves and lavender, pink, or white flowers
☼ Full light ⫤ In a container, no lower than 32°F (0°C) in winter Apply a balanced fertilizer every 4 weeks when in growth ⟳ Water freely when in growth, keep just moist in winter ⊞ Standard soil mix with added sand or perlite

Medinilla magnifica *Rose grape*
Height to 6ft (2m), spread 5ft (1.5m)
Exotic-looking shrubs with glossy, strongly ribbed leaves and showy, pink to coral-red flowers

Bright filtered light or full light with shade from hot sun ⫤ No lower than 59°F (15°C) in winter
In growth, apply a balanced fertilizer every 4 weeks Moderately when in growth, sparingly in winter ⊞ Standard soil mix

Monstera deliciosa *Swiss cheese plant*
Height to 10ft (3m), spread 3ft (1m)
This impressive foliage plant is actually a robust climber that can exceed the dimensions given if the conditions suit it
☼ Bright indirect light ⫤ No lower than 59°F (15°C) in winter In growth, apply a green houseplant fertilizer every 4 weeks ⟳ In growth, water freely and mist twice daily; water sparingly in winter ⊞ Standard soil mix

Narcissus hybrids *Daffodil*
Height to 14in (35cm), spread to 6in (15cm)
These delightful spring bulbs should be grown in containers outdoors and brought inside once the flower buds have formed
☼ Full light ⫤ No lower than 32°F (0°C) in winter
Apply a balanced fertilizer immediately after flowering ⟳ Water freely without flooding the compost ⊞ Standard soil mix or bulb fiber

Nephrolepis exaltata 'Bostoniensis' *Boston fern*
Height to 3ft (1m), spread 3ft (1m)
The Boston fern makes a tolerant houseplant, with fronds that are erect at first, then arch over
☼ Bright filtered light ⫤ No lower than 45°F (7°C) in winter In growth, apply a balanced fertilizer at half strength every 4 weeks ⟳ In full growth, water moderately with soft water and mist twice daily; water sparingly in winter ⊞ Standard soil mix with added sharp sand

Nertera granadensis *Bead plant*
Height to ¾in (2cm), spread 8in (20cm)
The principal attraction of this trailing plant is its shining, bead-like, orange or red berries that ripen in late summer
☼ Bright filtered or indirect light ⫤ No lower than 32°F (0°C) in winter In growth, apply a balanced fertilizer every 4 weeks ⟳ In growth, water freely, sparingly in winter ⊞ Soil-less potting mix

Ocimum basilicum *Basil*
Height to 12in (30cm), spread 12in (30cm)
This important culinary herb is essential for many Mediterranean, Indian, and Fusion dishes. It is generally grown as an annual
☼ Full light with shade from hot sun ⫤ No lower than 32°F (0°C) in winter Apply a balanced fertilizer when in growth ⟳ Water freely ⊞ Standard soil mix

Olea europea *Olive*

Height to 6ft (2m), spread 5ft (1.5m)

Familiar throughout the Mediterranean, where it is an important economic plant, the olive is an increasingly popular subject for a conservatory, though the olives are unlikely to ripen fully

☼ Full light ☷ Ideally no lower than 32˚F (0˚C) in winter, though short dry spells at lower temperatures are tolerated ♦ In growth apply a balanced fertilizer every 4 weeks ◊ Moderately when in growth, sparingly in winter ▨ Standard soil mix

Ophiopogon planiscapus 'Nigrescens'
Black grass

Height to 8in (20cm), spread to 12in (30cm)

This grass is a hardy plant that is grown for its unique, blackish purple leaves. It is best kept in a container outdoors and brought inside for short spells only

☼ Bright light with shade from direct sun ☷ Will tolerate lows of 5˚F (-15˚C) outdoors ♦ Apply a balanced fertilizer every 4 weeks when in growth ◊ Freely when in growth ▨ Standard soil mix

Origanum species *Marjoram, oregano*

Height and spread usually to 12in (30cm), but depends on the species

These aromatic herbs have wide culinary use as well as charming, lilac, pink, or mauve flowers

☼ Full light with shade from hot sun ☷ In a container, no lower than 32˚F (0˚C) in winter ♦ In growth, apply a balanced fertilizer every 4 weeks ◊ Moderately when in growth, sparingly in winter ▨ Standard soil mix

Paphiopedilum hybrids *Slipper orchid*

Height to 12in (30cm), spread 8in (20cm)

These orchids are becoming increasingly widely grown as houseplants and many attractive hybrids have been developed, most flowering in winter for up to 10 weeks or more

☼ Bright filtered light in summer; full light in winter ☷ No lower than 55˚F (13˚C) in winter ♦ In growth, apply an orchid fertilizer at every 3rd watering ◊ In growth, water freely and mist twice daily; in winter, water sparingly but do not allow the compost to dry out between waterings ▨ Terrestrial orchid potting mix in containers that restrict the roots

Pennisetum species *Fountain grass*

Height and spread to 24in (60cm), depending on species

Most of these grasses are hardy perennials that are best grown in containers outdoors and brought inside for short spells only

☼ Full light with shade from hot sun ☷ In a container, no lower than 32˚F (0˚C) in winter ♦ In growth, apply a balanced fertilizer every 4 weeks ◊ In growth, water freely, sparingly in winter ▨ Standard soil mix

Phalaenposis hybrids *Moth orchid*

Height to 3ft (1m), spread 2ft (60cm)

These beautiful orchids have been specially bred to tolerate the dry atmosphere of most centrally heated living rooms. The arching stems of flowers are of unmatched elegance and can be produced throughout the year. They are a popular choice for bridal bouquets

☼ Bright filtered light ☷ No lower than 64˚F (18˚C) in winter ♦ Apply an orchid fertilizer every 4 weeks from spring to autumn ◊ From spring to autumn, water freely and mist twice daily; in winter, water sparingly and do not mist ▨ Epiphytic orchid potting mix

Philodendron erubescens *Blushing philodendron*

Height to 6ft (2m), spread 12in (30cm), depending on how it is trained

This attractive climber has glossy, heart-shaped leaves. As a houseplant, it is best trained up a moss pole

☼ Bright filtered or indirect light ☷ No lower than 59˚F (15˚C) in winter ♦ In growth, apply a green houseplant fertilizer every 4 weeks ◊ Water freely when in growth, sparingly in winter ▨ Soil-less potting mix

Pogonatherum saccharoideum *House bamboo*

Height to 24in (60cm), spread 24in (60cm)

Most bamboos are large, colonizing plants, but the so-called house bamboo is an exception that makes a delightful houseplant

☼ Full light with shade from hot sun ☷ No lower than 59˚F (15˚C) in winter ♦ In growth, apply a balanced fertilizer every 4 weeks ◊ Water freely in active growth, only moderately in winter; the compost should never dry out ▨ Standard soil mix

Primula obconica *German primrose*

Height to 12in (30cm), spread 8in (25cm)

One of the prettiest of flowering houseplants for winter and spring, this primula is suitable for any cool area in the house such as a bedroom or hallway. The rough, hairy leaves can irritate the skin, so take care when handling

☼ Bright filtered light ☷ No lower than 32˚F (0˚C) in winter, though short spells at cooler temperatures are tolerated ♦ In growth, apply a balanced fertilizer at half strength every week ◊ Water freely when in growth, sparingly at other times ▨ Standard soil mix with added sand or perlite

Rosa hybrids *Rose*

Height to 4ft (1.2m), spread 3ft (1m), depending on the variety

Roses that are suitable for containers can be brought into the house for short spells as soon as the buds show color. After flowering, return them out of doors

☼ Full light with shade from hot sun ☷ In a container, no lower than 23˚F (-5˚C) in winter, though cooler temperatures can be tolerated ♦ Apply a balanced fertilizer when in growth ◊ Water freely when in growth; keep barely moist at other times ▨ Standard soil mix

Saintpaulia hybrids *African violet*

Height to 6–8in (15–20cm), spread 6–8in (15–20cm)

With clustered flowers in shades of white, pink, purple, magenta, and violet produced throughout the year, African violets are among the best flowering houseplants

☼ Bright filtered light ☷ No lower than 59˚F (15˚C) in winter ♦ Apply special Saintpaulia fertilizer throughout the year ◊ Water throughout the year to keep the soil moist and mist daily when in active growth ▨ Soil-less potting mix. Repot only when the roots fill the pot

Sansevieria trifasciata 'Laurentii'
Mother-in-law's tongue

Height to 3ft (1m), spread 12in (30cm)

With their boldly marked, upright leaves, these plants make a strong statement wherever they are placed

☼ Bright filtered or indirect light ☷ No lower than 55˚F (13˚C) in winter ♦ In growth, apply a balanced fertilizer at half strength every 4 weeks ◊ Freely when in full growth, sparingly in winter ▨ Standard soil mix with added sand

Schefflera elegantissima *False aralia*

Height to 6ft (2m), spread 3ft (1m)

This dramatic plant has strikingly toothed leaf margins

☼ Bright filtered or indirect light ☷ No lower than 55˚F (13˚C) in winter ♦ In growth, apply a balanced fertilizer every 4 weeks ◊ Moderately when in growth, keep just moist in winter ▨ Standard soil mix

Schlumbergera hybrids *Christmas cactus*

Height to 12in (30cm), spread 12in (30cm)

These rainforest cacti flower annually in autumn to winter when grown as houseplants, hence the common name

☼ Bright indirect light ☷ No lower than 50˚F (10˚C) in winter ♦ In growth, apply a flowering houseplant fertilizer every 4 weeks ◊ Water moderately when in full growth and mist daily; keep the soil just moist for up to 8 weeks after flowering to allow the plants to rest ▨ Epiphytic cactus soil mix

Scutellaria costaricana *Skullcap*

Height to 20in (50cm), spread 20in (50cm)

These shrubby plants produce spikes of fiery red flowers in summer. They have often been treated with a growth inhibitor to keep them compact for use as houseplants

☀ Bright filtered light ∦ No lower than 59°F (15°C) in winter ♦ In growth, apply a balanced fertilizer every 4 weeks ◊ Water freely when in growth, keep just moist in winter ▦ Standard soil mix

Senecio rowleyanus *String of beads*

Height to 24in (60cm), spread indefinite

This trailing plant, whose stems will root where they touch the soil surface, has spherical, bright green leaves. It is excellent in a hanging basket

☀ Full light ∦ No lower than 45°F (7°C) in winter ♦ In growth, apply a balanced fertilizer at half strength every 4 weeks ◊ Water moderately when in growth, keep just moist in winter ▦ Standard soil mix with added sand

Solanum pseudocapsicum *Jerusalem cherry*

Height to 12in (30cm), spread 12in (30cm)

These shrubs are grown for their marble-like, red, yellow, or orange fruits. They are often treated as annuals and discarded after fruiting

☀ Full light with shade from hot sun, or bright filtered light ∦ No lower than 41°F (5°C) in winter ♦ Apply a flowering houseplant fertilizer every 2–3 weeks until the fruits begin to ripen ◊ Water freely when in growth and mist daily; if not discarded, water sparingly when dormant after fruiting ▦ Standard soil mix

Soleirolia soleirolii *Baby's tears*

Height to 4in (10cm), spread indefinite

This spreading plant, with its tiny green leaves, is often used as ground cover in gardens. In pots, it makes appealing domes of foliage if several plants are massed together. Trim with scissors to keep neat

☀ Full light with shade from hot sun, or partial shade ∦ No lower than 32°F (0°C) in winter ♦ In growth, apply a balanced fertilizer at half strength every 4 weeks ◊ In growth, water freely, sparingly in winter ▦ Standard soil mix with added sand

Spathiphyllum wallisii *Peace lily*

Height to 36in (90cm), spread 36in (90cm)

These elegant plants produce their arum-like flowers throughout the summer

☀ Bright indirect light ∦ No lower than 50°F (10°C) in winter ♦ In growth, apply a balanced fertilizer every 4 weeks ◊ In growth, water freely and mist daily; keep just moist in winter ▦ Standard soil mix

Stephanotis floribunda *Floradora*

Height to 10ft (3m), spread 10ft (3m), depending on the support

These climbers, producing intoxicatingly scented flowers from spring to autumn, can be trained on hoops of wire inserted in the pot, or, where there is more room, on a trellis

☀ Full light with shade from hot sun ∦ No lower than 59°F (15°C) in winter ♦ In growth, apply a balanced fertilizer every 2–3 weeks ◊ In growth, water and mist freely; water sparingly in winter ▦ Standard soil mix

Tacca chantrierei *Bat flower, cat's whiskers, devil flower*

Height to 3ft (1m), spread 3ft (1m)

Among the huge, wrinkled leaves the sinister-looking green, brown, or black flowers, with thread-like appendages, make their appearance in summer

☀ Bright filtered light ∦ No lower than 55°F (13°C) in winter ♦ In summer, spray with a foliar fertilizer at half strength every 4 weeks ◊ Water and mist freely throughout the year ▦ Mix of leaf mold and coarse bark with added slow-release fertilizer

Thymus species *Thyme*

Height to 6in (15cm), spread to 12in (30cm), depending on the species

These aromatic sub-shrubs are grown mainly for culinary use, but also have the attraction of white, lilac, or purple flowers in summer, which are very attractive to bees. They can also be planted outdoors in the cracks in paving

☀ Full light ∦ In a container, no lower than 32°F (0°C) in winter, though short spells at cooler temperatures are tolerated ♦ In growth, apply a balanced fertilizer every 4 weeks ◊ In growth, water freely, moderately in winter ▦ Standard soil mix with added sand or perlite

Tillandsia wagneriana *Air plant*

Height to 16in (40cm), spread 18in (45cm)

This bromeliad is grown for its strap-like, curved, bright green leaves and its pink flowers, produced in spring or autumn

☀ Bright filtered light ∦ No lower than 45°F (7°C) in winter ♦ In growth, apply a flowering houseplant fertilizer at half strength every 4 weeks ◊ In growth, water freely; keep just moist in winter ▦ Terrestrial bromeliad soil mix

Tradescantia fluminensis 'Albovittata'

Wandering Jew

Height to 6in (15cm), spread 8in (20cm)

This familiar houseplant is easy to grow. Its trailing habit makes it ideal for massing in a hanging basket

☀ Bright filtered light ∦ No lower than 50°F (10°C) in winter ♦ In growth, apply a balanced fertilizer every 4 weeks ◊ In growth, water freely, sparingly in winter ▦ Standard soil mix

Tradescantia zebrina *Wandering Jew*

Height to 6in (15cm), spread 8in (20cm)

This trailing plant has pointed, bluish green leaves that are strongly striped with luminous silver. The three-petaled, purple-pink flowers, of lesser ornamental value, can be produced at any time during the year

☀ Bright filtered light ∦ No lower than 50°F (10°C) in winter ♦ In growth, apply a balanced fertilizer every 4 weeks ◊ In growth, water freely, sparingly in winter ▦ Standard soil mix

Viola x wittrockiana *Pansy*

Height to 9in (23cm), spread to 12in (30cm)

Pansies are universally popular with their mask-like "faces". They appreciate cool conditions, so keep them outdoors and bring them inside for short spells only. Plants are raised to flower at varying times of the year: winter-flowering pansies are especially welcome

☀ Full light with shade from hot sun ∦ Pansies will tolerate freezing temperatures ♦ Apply a flowering houseplant fertilizer every 2 weeks until the flower buds have formed ◊ Water freely, but avoid waterlogging the compost ▦ Standard soil mix

Vuylstekeara Cambria 'Plush'

Height to 4ft (1.2m), spread 2ft (60cm)

One of the least demanding orchids, this hybrid has tall, branching spikes of rust-red flowers that can appear at any time of year

☀ Bright filtered light when in active growth; full light in winter ∦ No lower than 50°F (10°C) in winter ♦ In growth, apply orchid fertilizer at every 3rd watering ◊ Water freely when in growth and mist twice daily; water sparingly in winter ▦ Epiphytic orchid potting mix

Zantedeschia hybrids *Calla lily*

Height to 36in (90cm), spread 24in (60cm)

Beautiful plants with shiny green leaves, flowering in spring to early summer. The elegant spathes (the true flowers inside are inconspicuous) are usually white, though yellow, pink, red, or purple varieties are also available. Some species are hardy and can be grown outdoors

☀ Full light ∦ No lower than 50°F (10°C) in winter ♦ In growth, apply a balanced fertilizer every 2 weeks until the flowers have faded ◊ In growth, water freely, keep just moist in winter ▦ Standard soil mix

USEFUL ADDRESSES

A M Leonard
tel 800 543 8955
Garden tools and supplies

Abundant Earth
762 West Park Avenue
Port Townsend
WA 98368
tel 360 385 2186
Organic gardening supplies

American Natural Products Co.
2103 185th Street
Fairfield
IA 52556-9232
tel 1 800 221 7645
Natural gardening products, including
fertilizers, insect control, disease `
control, etc.

Anthropologie
1801 Walnut Street
Philadelphia
PA 19103
tel 215 564 2313 (for branches)
Garden accessories, including a
range of pots and planters

Artemide
1980 New Highway
Farmingdale
NY 11735
tel 631 694 9292
www.artemide.com
Contemporary lighting

Asian Arts and Meditation Supplies
1813 Pearl Street
Boulder
CO 80302
tel 800 961 2555
www.chopa.com/ikebana.htm
Range of Oriental artifacts

Aveda
252 A Salon
2452 Broadway
New York
NY 10025
tel 212 875 1853
www.aveda.com
Scented candles

Bamboo Fencer, Inc.
179 Boylston Street
Jamaica Plain
MA 02130
tel 800 775 8641
www.bamboofencer.com
Garden furniture and accessories

Barbara Israel
21 East 79th Street
New York
NY 10021
tel 212 744 6281
Period garden furniture from Europe
and America

Bees Knees Garden Products
424 Narcissus
Corona del Mar
CA 92625
tel 800 834 8008
http://beesbotanical.com

Bloomingdales
1000 Third Avenue
New York
NY 10022
tel 212 705 2000
www.bloomingdales.com
Range of pots and containers

Brent and Becky's Bulbs
www.brentandbeckysbulbs.com
tel 877 661 2852

Chelsea Garden Center
321 Bowery
New York
NY 10003
tel 877 846 0565
www.chelseagardencenter.com
Handthrown terracotta and weathered clay pots

Classic Garden Products, Inc.
Pasadena
California
626 583-TEAK
www.TheClassicGarden.com
Garden accessories

Colonial Williamsburg
Department 023
PO Box 3532
Williamsburg
VA 23187-3532
tel 800 446 9240
Traditional garden accessories, candles
and tealights, other lighting

Cultus Bay Nursery
4000 E. Bailey Road
Clinton
WA 98236
tel 360 579 2329
Herbs

eGardenDepot.Com
www.egardendepot.com
Planters and general garden supplies

European Expressions
1301 N. Causeway Blvd.
Mandeville
LA 70471
French pottery from Provence

French Wyres
PO Box 131655
Tyler
TX 75713
tel 903 597 8322
Trellises, plant stands, and window boxes
made from fine wire

Gardener's Eden
PO Box 7307
San Francisco
CA 94120-7307
tel 800 822 9600 (for branches)
High-quality garden tools and
accessories

Historic Home Supply Corp
213–215 River Street
Troy
NY 12180-3809
tel 518 266 0675
www.homesupply.com
Reclaimed items, including garden accessories

Ikea
800 434 4532 (mail order)
www.ikea-usa.com
Range of pots and containers

Jackson and Perkins
1 Rose Lane
Medford
OR 97501
tel 541 776 2000
Roses

Johnny's Selected Seeds
305 Foss Hill Road
Albion
ME 04910
tel 207 437 9294 (mail order)
Variety of herbs

John Scheepers
23 Tulip Drive
Bantam
CT 06750
tel 860 567 0838
Bulbs

K-Mart
branches throughout the USA, ring
tel 800 866 0086 for nearest store
Plants in season, watering containers and other tools,
range of pots and containers

K. Van Bourgondien
245 Route 109
PO Box 1000
Babylon
NY 11702-9004
tel 516 669 3500
Bulbs

Lighting by Gregory
158 Bowery
New York
NY 10012
tel 212 226 1276
Selection of lighting from a variety
of manufacturers

L L Bean, Inc.
Freeport
ME 04033 0001
tel 800 441 5713
Range of garden accessories, including planters,
watering cans, candles, etc.

Macy's
420 Fulton Street
Brooklyn
New York
NY 11201-5214
tel 718 875 7200
www.macys.com
General range of pots and containers

New England Bamboo Company
5 Granite Street
Rockport
MA 01966
tel 978 546 3581
Bamboos and ornamental grasses

Noma Lights
Consumer Electrical Division
Wood Industries, Inc.
373 Kennedy Road
Scarborough
Ontario
Canada M1K 2AS
tel 416 267 4614
Leisure lighting

Norman's Orchids
11039 Monte Vista Ave.
Montclair
CA 91763
tel 909 627 9515

Old House Gardens
536 Third Street
Ann Arbor
MI 48103
tel 313 995 1486
Bulbs and tubers for spring flowers

Pahoa Orchids
PO Box 346
Pahoa
HI 96778
tel 808 965 9725
www.tropicalflower.com

Planet Natural
1612 Gold Avenue
Bozeman
MT 59715
tel 800 289 6656 or 406 587 5891
www.planetnatural.com
Organic fertilizers and other gardening supplies,
natural pest control

Plantitearth.Com
www.plantitearth.com
Hand-selected line of indoor gardening products,
including soils, plant foods, and containers

Pottery Barn
67th & Broadway
1965 Broadway
New York
NY 10023
tel 212 579 8477
and mail order
PO box 7044
San Francisco
CA 94120-7044
www.potterybarn.com
Range of pots and containers

Rio Grande Cacti
2188 NM Highway 1
Socorro
New Mexico 87801
www.riograndecacti.com

Roses.Com
806 Sam Houston Avenue
Huntsville
Texas 77320
www.roses.com
Roses, flowers, and houseplants
by mail order

Sandy Mush Herb Farm
316 Surret Cove Rd
Leicester
NC 28748
tel 828 683 2014
Scented-leaf pelargoniums

Seibert and Rice
PO Box 365
Short Hills
NJ 07078
tel 973 467 8266
Range of terracotta pots and containers

Serra Gardens
(not open to the public)
www.cacti.com
Cacti and succulents

Shady Hill Gardens
821 Walnut Street
Batavia
IL 60510
tel 630 879 5665

Smith and Hawken
2 Arbor Lane
PO Box 6900
Florence
KY 41022 6900
tel 800 776 3336 (for branches and mail order)
Good selection of plants and tools

The Candle Shop
tel 800-223-7201
www.candleexpress.com

Terrence Conran Shop
Bridgemarket
407 East 59th Street
New York
NY 10022
tel 212 755 9097
Range of pots and containers,
candles, lighting, etc.

The Herb Lady
52792 42nd Avenue
Lawrence
MI 49064

Troy
138 Greene Street
SoHo
New York
NY 10012
tel 212 941 4777
Reproduction furniture and ceramics

White Flower Farm
tel 800 503 9624
www.whiteflowerfarm.com

www.carsonbarnesorchids.com

GENERAL INDEX

ACKNOWLEDGMENTS

Author's Acknowledgments

I would like to thank the following for their help in creating *Hip Houseplants*: Vickie for her constant support; Jennifer d'Abo and the crew at Moyses Stevens for opening my eyes and allowing me to learn and develop; my assistant "Little Gem" thanks for being a "second pair of eyes" and for all those late nights; Jeremy Hopley, with assistants Liberty Silver and Rachel Warne, for the brilliant photography and supply of top-class CDs; Wei Tang for her innate sense of style; Doctor Frisbee and Doctor Thomas Johansen for the loan of their home.

The team from Dorling Kindersley: the dynamic duo, Judith More and Janis Utton, for their invaluable contribution; Neil Lockley for his patience and encouragement; Wendy Bartlet for all her hard work.

Also thanks to all at Arnott and Mason for their help with plants and verification; Craig of Quality Plants; Steve and Adam at H. Miles; C. Best for all the containers; the splendid Rob Cassy for all his advice.

Thank you to the following for the loan of various items: Aria for the black ceramic vases and fake fur throw on pages 24–25; ASA for containers on pages 10–11; Capital Garden Centre for the containers on pages 20–21 and the terracotta and stone pots on pages 22–23; Carden Cunietti for the cushions, throw, lampshade, stand, and set of boxes on pages 16–17, cushion, lampshade, stand, and small pony skin boxes on pages 24–25; Ceramica Blue for the large black tiles on pages 24–25; The Ivory Tower for the containers on pages 18–19, the large wooden urn containers and striped box on pages 24–25, and all items on pages 26–27; Kara Kara for the table on pages 16–17; Keith Brymer Jones for containers on pages 10–11 and for pages 28–29; Muji for the sofa on pages 16–17; Nimmo and Spooner for the large antique pots on pages 22–23; Nom for the tray, pot, large bamboo platter, and bowl on pages 16–17.

Publisher's Acknowledgments

Dorling Kindersley would like to thank Ann Parry for compiling the index.